YOUR CHILD'S WORLD

The Specific Approach to Daily Problems

Edited by Karl S. Bernhardt, Ph.D., Emeritus Director, Institute of Child Study, University of Toronto, and Everett Edgar Sentman, B.S., Editor in Chief, Tangley Oaks Educational Center.

This golden instant will never return. Only once will your child be two years old or four years old or at any other period of his growth. Only once will he live this moment, and his needs are of this moment. Now is the time—your child is waiting for you to *do something!* Monday morning's problems cannot be put off until Tuesday, or even until Daddy gets home. Life does not wait for the parent who quibbles or hesitates, who is always a book or chapter behind the imperative, constantly-changing *daily needs* of the child. YOUR CHILD'S WORLD is the book for busy parents. It brings you the best of today's advice on child guidance. Written by internationally known specialists, it offers a uniquely helpful organization of ninety-seven brief, easy-to-use articles. They're quick reading. You can find the answer to any of hundreds of child guidance problems in three to six minutes. With YOUR CHILD'S WORLD, the golden instant becomes a priceless opportunity to mold your child.

THE AUTHORS

George R. Bach
Staff psychologist,
Psycho-Education Clinic
University of Southern California
Los Angeles, California

Rhoda W. Bacmeister
Emeritus Director
Manhattanville Day Nursery
New York City

Mary L. Barrett, Ph.D.
Associate Professor of Child Development and Family Relationships
College of Home Economics
Cornell University
Ithaca, New York

Karl S. Bernhardt, Ph.D.
Emeritus Director,
Institute of Child Study
University of Toronto
Toronto, Ontario, Canada

Bettye M. Caldwell, Ph.D.
Research Associate
Department of Pediatrics
Upstate Medical Center
Syracuse, New York

Tess Cogen
Family Life Education Director,
The Association for Family Living,
Chicago

Edith Ford
Curriculum Director
Park Ridge (Ill.) Public Schools

Elizabeth Mechem Fuller, Ph.D.
Institute of Child Welfare
University of Minnesota
Minneapolis, Minnesota

Dale B. Harris, Ph.D.
Head of Department of Psychology
Pennsylvania State University
University Park, Pennsylvania

James L. Hymes, Jr., Ph.D.
Professor of Education
George Peabody College for Teachers
Nashville, Tennessee

Lester A. Kirkendall, Ph.D.
Professor of Family Life Education
Oregon State University
Corvallis, Oregon

1

THE AUTHORS—*Continued*

Margaret Rohner Lindman

Principal, College Hill School
Evanston, Illinois, District 65
Lecturer in Education, Loyola University
Elementary School Teacher (1950-57)
Teacher of Literature, Drama, and
  Speech
National College of Education (1957-64)
Tangley Oaks Advisory Editor

Edith E. Maddox

Kindergarten Teacher
Palos Verdes Estates, California

Ralph K. Meister, Ph.D.

Director, Mooseheart Laboratory
  for Child Research
Mooseheart, Illinois

Lucy Nulton, Ph.D.

P. K. Yonge Laboratory School
College of Education
University of Florida
Gainesville, Florida

Bonaro W. Overstreet

Education Specialist;
Collaborator with Husband,
  Harry Overstreet, on Books
  About Emotional Security

Douglas F. Parry, Ph.D.

Professor of Education and Psychology
Director of Remedial Services
Texas A. & M. University System
College Station, Texas

Angelo Patri

Noted Child-Care Specialist and Writer

Josephine A. Piekarz

Assistant Director, Reading Clinic
University of Chicago
Chicago, Illinois

Blaine M. Porter, Ph.D.

Chairman of Department
  of Human Development and
  Family Relationships
Brigham Young University
Provo, Utah

Martha Ransohoff

Lecturer on Child Care and Training
College of Home Economics
University of Cincinnati
Cincinnati, Ohio

Arthur L. Rautman, Ph.D.

Chief Clinical Psychologist
Mental Hygiene Service
Veterans Administration Regional Office
St. Petersburg, Florida

Katherine Reeves, Ph.D.

Professor of Child Development and
  Family Relationships
State College of Home Economics
Cornell University
Ithaca, New York

Marguerita Rudolph

Fresh Meadows (N.Y.) Nursery School
Author of "Living and Learning
  in Nursery School"

Alfred Schmieding, LL.D.

Chairman of Department of Education
  and Psychology, and Academic Dean
Concordia Teachers College
River Forest, Illinois

Robert H. Seashore, Ph.D.

Professor of Psychology
Northwestern University
Evanston, Illinois

Everett Edgar Sentman

Editor in Chief
Tangley Oaks Educational Center
Encyclopedia Builder and Author

Ruth Strang, Ph.D.

Professor of Education
University of Arizona
Tucson, Arizona

Lovisa Wagoner, Ph.D.

Professor of Child Development
Mills College
Oakland, California

Mary Cooper Walton

Nursery-School Specialist
Wellesley College
Wellesley, Massachusetts

Paul A. Witty, Ph.D.

Professor of Education
Northwestern University
Evanston, Illinois

Copyright 1955, 1960, 1961, 1963, 1965, 1967 by
THE BOOK HOUSE FOR CHILDREN
Lake Bluff, Illinois 60044

Made in United States of America

Table of Contents

Table of Contents—*Continued*

Library of Congress catalog number 67-27967
ISBN 0-87566-006-1

The Creative Home

By KATHERINE REEVES

The home, someone has said, is the last stronghold of freedom in the modern world. This is a rather terrifying thought, and at the same time an exciting and stimulating one. It says to us that the home can experiment in the direction of a society where everyone can be his best and happiest and most effective self; that the home can find out what kinds of experience make for the development of creative people, who in turn make living a great, affirmative enterprise among men.

Perhaps no two people would describe the creative home in the same way. We should have first to agree on what "creative" means. All we can do, individually, is say, *"to my way of thinking* these are the distinguishing qualities of the creative home."

1. *The creative home gives its children living room.* This is necessary physically and emotionally. Increasingly, home planning is taking into account the fact that children need space in which to act and think and feel. The creative home is not necessarily the home that can provide a rich material environment. It may be that kind. There is no reason why a luxurious home should not be a creative one as well. But there is also no reason why the most modest and simple physical environment cannot at the same time be the setting for the most creative living. The creative spirit resides in the human heart, not in the pine paneled suburban house or the city tenement, nor any conventional dwelling in between. Living room for the body is important, but living room for the spirit is essential, so—

2. *The creative home is one in which a certain kind of positive relationship is always at work.* This is a freeing, strengthening, quickening relationship. There is in it an absence of tyranny, an overflowing abundance of love and a liberating goodwill, which make it possible for the real concerns of every family member to have consideration.

Ewing Galloway

3. *The creative home makes daily living a gracious thing:* The best table silver and the best manners are for the family. The routines of homemaking become as important as mastering a piano score, or taking the lead in the school play, because they are thought of that way. Consideration becomes a habit, because it is given, and received, at home.

4. *The creative home allows exploration:* The insatiable and natural curiosity of the young child must be fed by a multitude of experiences which permit him to use his senses, even though mud gets tracks on the carpet now and then, or a dish gets broken. The curiosity and zest of the older child must also be fed. It is the home, best of all, which can give a child the chance to try out his own abilities and improve his skills; which can give him warm appreciation for his halting, inept, and sometimes inconvenient efforts to find out about himself; which can be patient with his inexperience; which can subordinate a desire for perfection to the growth-value of the child's doing. A home which does these things enables a child to form a true image of himself, one of the great tasks of any age we are told.

5. *The creative home puts just and consistent limits on behavior:* A child is entitled to guidance. When he knows what the limits are, and the reasons for them, he is saved from useless dissipation of energy and vital power in the struggle to find them. And as a child grows the creative home allows him to make some of the rules and to have a part in decisions which affect him. By helping a child understand and accept reasonable limits the home not only helps him know himself, but fortifies him as he tries to discover and fulfill his special place in his social group.

6. *The creative home gives support and nourishment to emotional health:* It is concerned as fully with emotional health as with physical, knowing that the two are parts of a whole, not separate entities; knowing that a stomachache and a heartache are often the same thing. In the home, and only in the home, feelings can be freely expressed and hostility brought out into the open without fear of punishment or penalty.

7. *The creative home tries to make the child "at home in the world":* One family achieved this in the course of a trip by trailer across the continent. The fellowship of the trailer camp at nightfall, the brief but positive contacts between families and among children of all levels of endowment and purpose gave the children in this family a never-to-be-lost sense of the extent and diversity of family life. Understanding and acceptance of people in general, not just the familiar people on the home street, is a goal of great importance. But first must come the achievement of that goal within the family group.

8. *The creative home knows that there are infinite facets to human experience:* It is important to know how to earn a living, but it is also important to know how to live a rich and brimming life. Education and training which accomplishes one and ignores the other is short-changing the child.

9. And perhaps the greatest of all characteristics of the creative home is its *recognition of the needs of children for a chance to discover themselves* and to find that blend of freedom and social responsibility which will make them good and happy citizens of the home, the community, and that larger neighborhood—the world.

Too Many Dreams

By JAMES L. HYMES, JR.

Do you dream big dreams for your children? Parents do. We see our one-year-old son as a business man one day, working and successful; our daughter of three as a happy mother with children of her own; our seven-, a famous teacher, loved and respected, helping real children instead of dolls; our nine-, as a hero on the football field and diamond. It is all there for them—college, a home, honor, fame . . . all in our mind's eye.

This is part of the glory of America: we are free to dream. And it is part of the glory of today — these dreams can come true. We live in a bubbling world, a changing and developing world. Yesterday's wild dreams are today's commonplace.

All parents do it. But some of us do it more than others—perhaps the more ambitious ones of us—we dare to hope for the very best for our young. Perhaps the more earnest of us, and the wiser and more prudent

—look to the future, make ready for it and plan ahead. This is good Twentieth Century Americanism.

It is the basis for insurance and savings accounts and retirement benefits; it gives us cars and homes and hospital care when we need it. But it may not give us happy children. These dreams can have pitfalls in them. This looking only at the future is not *all* wise for children.

Children have to live each *today*. They have to *be* two and five and nine; they cannot always live in a state of *be*-coming. Children need acceptance and support and encouragement for what they are now. It is not enough to have hopes for what they can do *someday*.

Our dreams can fool us into forgetting this. Our dreams can weary our eyes for life here and now because we are straining them to see the life far ahead. We can come to think always of our children as "pre" . . . as *pre*-dry babies, *pre*-talkers, *pre*-walkers, *pre*-readers . . . as not grown now but getting ready for something good.

The more your eye is on the future, the more you want to hurry today, to get it over with. "I'll be glad when my child can talk." "I'll heave a sigh of relief when my child can walk." "Will the time ever come when I will be able to leave him alone at night?" Always the good thing is over the horizon; today they are just "pre."

We begin to bring pressure on them—all out of our good hopes and our high ideals. "Pick up your room," we say. And we think not of our six- but of a twenty-six-, a future good husband or wife. "Is he reading yet?" we anxiously ask. And we think not of our first-grader but of a man or woman twenty years from now. "Don't dawdle so," we nag, and it is not today that bothers us but the vision of some slow-pokey tomorrow.

We begin to limit what they can do. We narrow down the field to what really counts. "Don't play; you have to practice your piano," but whom do we have in mind? Not our real seven-year-old but the seventeen-year-old she will someday become. "Leave your blocks alone now and do your job" and we are really talking, not to a playful five- but to a dream - adult who "ought" to be serious.

It can change our whole perspective. It blinds us to where children have been and to how far they have come. Always, all we can see is that long, long way they still have to go. "You've torn your pants again;

won't you ever learn to take care of your things?" . . . "You've spilled your soup. When are you going to learn to do things right?" . . . "Such language for a child to use!" . . . and we forget that not so long ago they hit and spit and pulled hair when they were mad. Progress doesn't interest us because our eyes are on the future.

Play, experimentation, interests, first steps to independence—none of these seems important now. Always the values are in tomorrow.

Our own better nature can do it to us.

Our own love for our children.

Our fine hopes for their measuring up and getting the best out of life.

There are pitfalls in dreaming. But if we know it we can guard against them. We can help our children live in this today and live well. And we can know that this is not being careless. This is not "throwing the baby out with the bath." This is planning and prudence but it is psychologically sound.

For to accept three-year-olds as they are—or youngsters of any age; to enjoy children as they are; to help them live happily as threes- (or as fives- or nines-)—this *does* build for the future but in a wise way. For the best preparation that a child can have for tomorrow is to live well today. Tomorrow counts, but it will be a good tomorrow only if it is grounded on happy todays.

- - - and Speaking of Dreams - - -

A young couple stood, happily looking down upon their first-born son, lying in his crib asleep. As the mother gazed down on the little year-old tot, she saw him growing up—in her mind's eye. She saw him going to school, becoming a great student. She saw him studying law, trying important cases. She saw him becoming a senator, an ambassador—and finally she pictured herself in the White House, the mother of the President!

Then she turned to look thoughtfully at her husband. She wondered what he had been thinking as he looked at his son—and she asked him.

The husband, smiling a little at his wife's curiosity, replied: "He's such a little fellow—I wonder if he can stand up under a third term." —MAGAZINE DIGEST

FEELING CLOSE TO MOTHER is important to the young child. Later, mother must recognize the signs of growing independence.

Ewing Galloway

Security Begins At Home

By BONARO W. OVERSTREET

Skill Is a Firm Foundation

While we were lunching with a friend one day, and talking about various projects that lay close to her heart, my husband put to her a question that we had already, in private, put to each other with regard to her: "How did you get to be the way your are?"

In more expanded form the question might have been phrased, "What experiences in your past can be held happily accountable for the generous integrity of your present relationship to life?" For that was what we wanted to know.

There she sat with us at the table —talking to her two almost-grown sons, both of them headed with love into the teaching profession; talking of her community, of education, of mental health, of citizens learning to feel the creative strength of their citizenship; laughing with us about the high absurdities of humankind; sorrowing with us over the squandered resources of men; fearing with us the consequences of too much fear in the world. Through all her words there ran a sure current of warmth, affection, courage, humor. How did she get to be that way? We wanted to know. . . .

Her answer when it came started with a sentence that was at once biologically obvious and psychologically significant: "Well . . . I had parents. . . ."

Then she put together for us, out of vivid pieces of memory, the picture of her mother who had given her an initial slanting toward life: "There were three things mother felt every woman should know— how to cook expertly, and with joy;

how to conduct a meeting according to *Robert's Rules of Order;* and how to arrange flowers with the skill of a professional."

She told other things, too—about her father, for example, who had been a strong force for political integrity in his town and state; and who had, during her childhood, been friend and host to the finest minds and spirits who came his way.

But all the while she talked, one fact kept its central place: namely, *that her parents had set high value on the skills of life.* They had not, sentimentally, thought it enough to have good intentions. In the phrase of Father Jimmy Tompkins, of Nova Scotia, they had known that "ideas have hands and feet." The skills of preparing a meal, of welcoming guests, of making a home beautiful, of discussing social and political problems, of organizing community movements—all of these were to be incorporated in what they saw as the necessary equipment for a life that was to be at once happy and useful.

And across from us at the table sat their physical and spiritual daughter: a woman competently at home in her world who could bring both grace and honor to the handling of personal and community problems. Hers, we saw, as she talked, was the goodly heritage of a double wisdom: wisdom about what is worth doing, and wisdom about how to do it excellently.

II

L. P. Jacks, the noted English adult educator, has described us human beings as "skill-hungry." It is a good word to apply. The more we learn about our own nature, the more apparent it becomes that our proper activity is that of reaching out toward the realities of our world: reaching out with affection, curiosity about the make-up of things, appreciation, resourcefulness, creative ingenuity, accurate knowledge, wide-ranging interest. The defeated human, we are beginning to realize, is the one who, by reason of one emotional block or another, rejects his role as a creature of outreach. He withdraws from reality and lives with fictions of his own making: sees dangers where no actual dangers exist; dreams himself into heroic roles that he never acts out in the objective world; exaggerates the difference between himself and others; shuns situations that put him to the test. Too inept in his handling of reality to be the master of circumstances, he is exaggeratedly the victim of circumstances.

The normal risks of outreach become abnormally terrifying where the individual does not know how to do well any of the things through which he might make himself felt as a person; establish his significance and worth.

III

In our complex modern society, our major skills—our vocational and even our recreational skills—are brought to their maturity outside the home: in school and college and on the job, but this fact in nowise lessens the responsibility of the home. For the child who goes off to school for the first time and the grown-up who goes to work for the first time are alike in one vital respect: they both carry with them into the new situation certain basic attitudes they acquired at home; and these attitudes will be a major reason why they do or do not make

Beatrice and Jules Pinsley

the most of the learning opportunities they face.

The home still is the place, in brief, where the foundations of future confidence and competence are laid. They are likely to be soundly laid if the parents in the home have themselves a fine respect for craftsmanship and a contagious joy in their own work; if each child is encouraged by interest and approval to try his hand at the arts of outreach; if each child is given a chance to fumble and fail and succeed without being hurried, humiliated, laughed at for the legitimate clumsiness of his learning, unfavorably compared with other children.

To love and to learn: these, we begin to know, are the two great prerequisites to human happiness. And no small part of learning is *learning how*: learning how to do with body and mind the many things that add up to a self-respecting good-will relationship with life.

The child who, in the home, is given both a chance to *learn how* and an example of the satisfaction that comes from *knowing how* may well, in his adult years, explain his deep happiness as our friend explained hers: "Well . . . I had parents. . ."

11

Gifts of a Very Good Mother — Time

By LUCY NULTON

In "Once Upon a Time," *that magic realm of fairyland, the princess was endowed by fairy godmothers with gifts precious and rare. As with all fairy tales, therein lay truth, apparently magic, but hard truth—the foundation of our world of reality. It is true that every mother may give to her child the gifts which would be the envy of a fairy godmother. These are gifts of beauty and lifelong value which every good mother gives to her child through the daily way of life chosen with and for her family.*

Child overheard meditating aloud: "Day before tomorrow Mommie took me to Grandmamma's. At Grandmamma's there isn't 'any We-don't-have-time-to-do-that . . . Grandmamma doesn't have a watch on her arm . . . At Grandmamma's I feel good."

In the child's world, time is not measured grudgingly. Time is *now*. Time is being.

The young child has slight conception of time, immediate or historical. He has no perspective of experience by which to measure time. Therefore, there are some very vital things which the little child needs from adults in relation to time.

He needs the adult's understanding that when he is happily engrossed in what he is doing, for him time goes on and on. There is no end. So we do not jerk him suddenly away from what he is doing. We give him a few minutes' warning ahead of time and allow him to get adjusted to the idea that there comes an end to the happi-est of engrossing experiences. (After all, none of us likes to be yanked away from something on which we are happily concentrated!) We help him to *look forward* to the next experience, matter-of-factly if it is routine, joyously if it is exploration.

We must continuously plan the day with the child's needs in mind. We did this when he was a young infant, physically helpless. It is no less important now, though his needs are of a different kind.

If Mother needs certain time to get a necessary thing done, she can plan for or with the child an activity which requires comparable time, and which will hold his interest.

When a child must share Mother's activities, such as going to the grocery store, mother must allow a longer time, knowing that the child's rate of speed is not as fast as an adult's. Then Mother can relax and enjoy the child's happiness.

Beatrice and Jules Pinsley

We must plan for alternating periods of energetic, and quiet activities. We watch the child's participation and get a clue to how long each period should last. As in eating and sleeping, he will set up his own wholesome rhythms if we but study him and adapt to his rhythm.

We accept the fact that each person is geared to his own speed. In the world there is a valued place for each speed. We cannot change the gearing of a person; to try to do so causes serious upsets of personality, capability, balance.

Understanding that the child has no sense of time, we must deliberately help him develop one. We mention the hour when the big, important things in his life happen. "Daddy comes home at five." "Billy has orange juice at ten o'clock." "Sleepy time at . . ." As he grows older, we mention the clock. We learn the days of the week by singing the song, chanting the days , enumerating things we do on certain days. We let him listen to an old clock which he can hold; let him watch the hour glass timing the eggs. We use expressions which help: "Once upon a time Billy was a baby. That was four years ago." "When mother was a little girl . . ."

We realize and accept that the little child needs longer to accomplish an undertaking than an adult. He has few habits established to help him accomplish anything quickly. He has poor coordination and is apt to have difficulty in manipulation of objects. If he is quite young, he is easily distracted; his attention goes elsewhere. He tires easily.

We value the fact that it is the serious, developmental business of the young child to find out about things. Consequently, he often has side interests which take time. Instead of going straight to the swing when he steps out, as Mother had thought he was going to do, he stops to pat the cat. He pulls off the head of a flower and crams it into his mouth. He throws up both arms and utters gibberish at a plane flying overhead. Eventually he may get to the swing. Meanwhile, he has experienced sensations of touch, taste, sight, hearing, smell, and has responded to some of them with his own talk or other means of expression. He now knows more about the world in which he lives. It is his business to learn these things. It takes time— uninterrupted time.

So we allow him to take time. We take time ourselves—to play with him, to talk to him, to enjoy companionship with him. We take time to talk clearly, distinctly, quietly, with varying modulations of tone. It is worth it! Time is such that we will never have this precious childhood period again.

Carefully we guard our lips that we never say, "Hurry, dear. Hurry!"

Every person, from infancy to ninety, needs some time of his own. Every person has a right to some time of his own, uninterrupted and unintruded-upon. Therefore, we shall not crowd the child's day full, even of enjoyable and valuable experiences. We shall not enslave him to a crowded schedule which allows him no time for being a child.

The complexity and speed of this era are making timing a technique of deep importance in the whole matter of human relations, and the way we get along with people. Recognizing this and striving to understand the child's needs, we realize that *time* is one of the child's most valuable gifts from the very good mother of our era.

Gifts of a Very Good Mother

PRIVACY OF SOUL

By LUCY NULTON

A gift of rarest delicacy between persons of close relationship is that of each allowing the other his own inner spirit, unintruded upon and unprobed.

Every child, even as every adult, has the right to live without being "picked" and probed to expose his every thought and his most personal feelings.

"Mummy," said very young Jon, laying a battered old box carefully on his bookshelf, "this is my secret treasure box. Please don't let anyone touch it."

"All right," Mummy answered cheerfully, adding carefully within her own spirit, "my littlest angel."

Nor was the box touched until Jon returned to it three days later.

Out of such acceptance of the child's right to secret things, to treasures all his own, uninvestigated and untarnished by adult handling, comes to the child a relaxed sense of personal integrity which makes him a whole and wholesome person.

Only at great risk dare we intrude upon the feelings which cause any person to carry around with him some treasure of special meaning—a piece of colored glass, a faded "sweet Betsy" bud, a knot out of a board, a dry and lifeless grasshopper with red underwings, a portrait of one's wife, prayer beads, a pocket Bible.

There even comes a time when the child may carry a book everywhere he goes, looking into it perhaps rarely, scarcely able to read, but carrying it lovingly.

What meaning does this thing he carries have for him? We do not know. We do not probe, pry, question, or hound him about his feeling, trying to get him to tell us what is in the book or box. The insensitive question that adults frequently bludgeon a child with, "*Why* do you like that?" is unanswerable. Usually he doesn't know why. (Do adults always know their whys?) Occasionally a child may know why, yet he may have a very personal feeling which he needs to protect, untouched, until he can explore it further or savor to its fullest its special meaning for him alone. To try to force communication may cause dishonesty. To have to talk too much or too soon may deaden sensibilities, dull curiosity, cause the growth of a deep resentment, or foster feelings of shame and guilt.

For privacy of soul (his and ours), let us all avoid, like the disease that it is, nagging at a person to try to gain information, trying to penetrate and possess his feelings, or attempting to keep him from practicing what *we* consider an undesirable habit.

"You're the bestest Mother," sighed seven-year-old Rose contentedly. "You don't ever go running around all-the-time-talking about me."—a long, quiet pause.—"I love you, Mother."

Let us honor the child's confidence when he chooses to share himself with us, keeping with deepest respect— even with extra precautions against violation — this spirit, knowledge, longing, or observation he feels comfortable in bestowing upon us. We do not share it with others. Confidings are not coins to be passed on.

Ethyl Corporation

attempts without laughing at them, without trying to improve them, without patronizingly calling them "cute" or "funny."

The calling of such names, too, intrudes upon the child's personality, prevents his being himself, burdens him with an unwholesome self-consciousness, makes him something less than a human being.

Genuine understanding allows, without intruding, the very delicate, deeply personal moments of another's life. Perhaps it may be when he makes up a new "inside song," discovers beauty, creates an imaginary person, loses a pet, comes face to face with the period of death. Into such moments we cannot tread unasked.

Nor do we search our children for unworthy motives. Only as we believe in the child, recognizing and respecting his capabilities, his growing potentialities, his worthiness, and his unique personality, do we help him grow within himself a personal strength.

If we genuinely respect him, we do not laugh *at* a child—his worries, ideas, expressions, or his immature attempts to accomplish something. A child's crude poem, laughed at, leaves a maimed and muted spirit. He will take care that no one invade his privacy again. In that defensiveness, something of his spirit dies. He becomes humdrum, his life dull.

Often easy, friendly silence creates a feeling of confidence—one can be sure enough of the other person to dare question, conjecture, dream dreams aloud. Besides, it is in such relaxed, friendly silence that creation takes place, dreams take form.

So it comes, this privacy of soul which makes a person healthy, through the knowledge that the grown-ups in one's world can go adventuring. They can accept one's own adventures and curiosity. They can value ideas and

Out of a far flight of fancy in a big, red airplane, Little Girl heard Mother calling her to supper. The swing stopped. Little Girl paused to say gracious words of good-by to her plane hostess.

She was a few minutes late getting to the table, but Mother's smile welcomed her. In the relaxation of that understanding smile she explained. "Mother, I've just come back from a long trip. The plane went 'way, 'way high! The hostess was so pretty and kind, Mother. She looked just like you!"

"Thank you, dear, and thank you for telling me about your trip," Mother answered casually. "I'm glad you had a good time."

Mother had given readily and generously her recognition of Little Girl's right to the privacy of her own soul.

15

"My Daddy Knows Everything"

By EVERETT E. SENTMAN

WHEN people at a party ask, "And what do you do?" and I have to confess I am an encyclopedia editor, they toss me one of those "that tears it" smiles and trot off in search of more interesting companions, such as a newspaper reporter (which I once was) or a Texas millionaire (which I will never be).

This has happened often enough to move me to try to avoid adult parties. I'll take my tea and mud pies with the dolls.

Being an encyclopedia editor may cut no cake with grownups, but it certainly gives a man status with kids. Somebody else's Pop may have a thirty-inch television screen or a record of winning touchdowns, and almost anybody's parents make more money. But an encyclopedia editor *knows everything*.

The obvious rejoinder, that nobody knows everything, has nothing to do with the case. We are dealing here, not with cold facts, but with the delicately-balanced relationships between a man and his public. This particular public starts at home and runs down both sides of the street,

shrieking and shooting off cap pistols.

My reputation got its start with my own kids. I well remember the day when Sheila, with a woman's instinct for accurate sources of information, turned to me instead of her mother and asked, "Daddy, where does the sun sleep at night?" My heart leaped. This was the moment for which I had toiled through months of nocturnal bottle warming, ringing changes on diapers and catching a high fly of cereal in right field with the bases loaded.

Taking her spinachy little hand in mine, I answered her question in a few well-chosen words suited to her level of comprehension. It may have been a father's foolish fancy, but I thought I saw a gleam of filial pride in her eyes. I was sure of it at four o'clock the next morning when she awakened me instead of her mother to have her sleepers unbuttoned.

But such victories are not won at a single stroke. Sheila had me tentatively tagged as a brain, but she had to make sure I could last the stretch. During the next several weeks she tested me at odd moments. While shaving, I was called upon to explain why Mommy doesn't have a mustache. While mowing the lawn, "Daddy, why is the grass green?" While stumbling to Baby's crib with a glass of water by the light of a first-quarter

moon, "Daddy, why is the moon broken? Can you fix it?"

Well, naturally, the things you learn while editing an encyclopedia come to your aid at times like these. Father batted 1.000.

Sheila began asking me to button her dress in back and to perform other little personal chores that a woman reserves for the man of her choice. She took me on long walks with her tricycle and introduced me to the neighbors. When she said "My Daddy," she capitalized it.

Her mother, an indulgent woman, said none of the things she might have said to dampen this romance.

By the time our second daughter came along, I was mad with power and lusting for more. I couldn't wait for Sue to learn to talk so she could ask me questions. To arouse her interests in the world of knowledge, I presented her with simple, question-provoking situations in pantomine. I set up problems in blocks and dolls, and then solved them deftly. But for a long time all I got was an amused stare that suggested I wasn't any brighter than I should be.

After she did learn to talk, *she* told *me* things. Apparently she had been saving them up for a long time. She developed, and related to me, 16 different versions of "Goldilocks and the Four Bears." There were four bears because, to Sue, family life was inconceivable without a Big Sister for Little Bear. But she showed absolutely no respect for her own immediate male forebear.

When I waggled my mustache at her, hoping she would ask why Mommy was not blessed with this adornment, she insisted that I shave it off. This I did, to the accompaniment of sotto voce wifely jibes about "Who is the head of the house now?" Once the deed was done, Sue cried because I looked funny. For a week or so in midsummer my upper lip gave the appearance of having spent a long vacation under a log.

I am happy to report, however, that Sue finally started asking me questions. She just couldn't hold out against daily association with genius.

Meanwhile Sheila, now at school, had announced to her teacher, "My Daddy is an encyclopedia editor."

"Oh, how nice," smiled Teacher vaguely and changed the subject. You see what I mean about adults.

After a pregnant silence Baby let her have it. "My DADDY knows EVERYTHING!" This got Sheila's educational career off to a fine start, and made her father the butt of ribaldry in the P.T.A.

I should have known that a gift like knowing everything cannot long remain hidden in the bosom of the family, modest though the omniscient one may be. My larger public began to form.

One Sunday afternoon I looked up from my paper to find myself surrounded by a platoon of little boys

and girls, all eyeing me intently. Sue jabbed one of them toward me and said, "Oh, go on, Joe, ask him."

After a few manly tugs at his playsuit, Joe cleared his throat and asked, "Mr. Sentman, what would happen if you tore a great big hole in the sky?"

Tough question? Easy as falling off a log. You simply explain the aerodynamics of a rocket flying at supersonic speed. Suffice it to say that my new-found admirers spent the afternoon blasting off to the stratosphere.

Before long, kids I had never seen before detoured past my chair to ask me questions on their way to the bathroom. Sample question: "Why is a caterpillar squishy inside?" With this one a crudely but thoroughly dissected specimen was deposited right in my lap.

Occasionally one of my stimulating fact-packed dissertations took longer than the questioner had anticipated. The third or fourth time this happened my wife suggested rather spiritedly that I send my seekers-after-knowledge to the bathroom *first*.

Don't think it is easy maintaining a reputation as the man who knows everything. Some of my public is beginning to grow up and take an interest in things like nuclear physics.

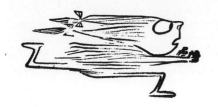

I've got a fledgling ornithologist who has given me some bad moments. Bird watching has never been my forte.

Keeping up with these kids takes some night work with — you guessed it — the encyclopedia. But the satisfaction is worth it. Children love knowledge, and they'll love you, too, if you dish it out when they ask for it. Just use simple, straightforward talk and don't condescend, because they can spot a phony every time. Give them examples and illustrations from their own everyday experience. Don't force your wisdom on them. Just answer the question and then shut up. You'll find, as I have found, that it's more fun to be a big wheel with kids than a slick raconteur among a flock of adults who, after all, already know everything.

Reprinted by kind permission of
Parents' Magazine; copyright 1953 by Parents Institute

PUTTING FATHER ON THE SPOT. This is Sue's impression of her Pop preparing to devastate his small inquisitors. She knows that if he doesn't have the answer to their question, he can find it in the encyclopedia.

What it Means to be a Good Parent

by KARL S. BERNHARDT

BEING a good parent is a real challenge, for it is something that does not just happen. It requires effort and study, and it requires cultivation of a number of attitudes and personality traits. It takes love, patience, clear objectives, intelligence, skill and knowledge. Here are some aspects of parental love which need to be discussed.

An important feature of child training is the provision of a basis for the feeling of belonging, being wanted, accepted and loved. The child who does not feel wanted and loved is the child who is likely to develop emotional quirks and to present behavior problems which may be difficult to deal with. But loving one's children does not mean either indulgence and spoiling or using affection as a means of control. The two main functions of parenthood, affection and discipline, should be kept separate and distinct. This is not easy. It is easy to use affection as a tool of control or as a reward for good behavior. But this can both cheapen affection and make discipline less than adequate. Parents should love their childen—by all means—but not depending on good behavior. Parental love should stand as a solid unchanging background of parent-child relations.

Happy is the child who feels that he is wanted and loved—happy because he is living in an atmosphere conducive to healthy learning and development.

Mothers and fathers are partners who can help each other by taking time to discuss their hopes and fears, their plans and techniques, and so gain clear ideas, more objective attitudes, and better plans for dealing with the everyday problems of parenthood.

Being a good parent requires patience, for it take time for a child to learn. Part of the parent's job is to arrange opportunities for learning, and then to allow the child to go about it himself. The rhythm of a child's activity is not as rapid as that of an adult, nor his muscular control as well developed. Adults with young children frequently lose patience and attempt to hurry them in such situations as dressing, washing and eating, and this often gives rise to the unfortunate habit of adults dealing with children—the habit of nagging.

A realization is needed that a child is naturally slow and awkward in his movements, for he is learning and cannot be expected to be as efficient as he will be later. Do not expect too much too soon. It takes a long time to produce an adult and the five-year old should not be expected to act like one.

Parental patience is needed in the inevitable comparisons of one's own child with other's. Family pride is involved, for when a parent hears that a neighbor's child is developing faster than his own, he is tempted to blame or try to hurry him. Children differ greatly in their tempo of learning and developing. Comparisons are dangerous and family pride can be an enemy of effective child training.

Know what you want the child to learn and why. In deciding the best

21

course to follow, it is well to decide first what the end result is to be and what kind of a person we are trying to produce. When a long-range view is taken we tend to select methods which aid in the learning and development of the child. I would suggest that it is necessary to consider as a goal, the production of a well-adjusted adult. When we think in terms of the present only, we tend to use methods for immediate results. We want an individual who is self-disciplined, capable of running his own life satisfactorily, and capable of adjusting to an ever-changing world.

Know how children learn. To learn, there has to be a reason, and the most dependable motives of study are the child's own needs and wants. He must put forth effort, taste success and failure, and discover what works and what does not. Learning is most efficient when the end results of effort are immediate and consistent, so the parent should keep consistence in mind—always the same result following the same kind of behavior.

Take pains to arrange for the child to learn how to decide things for himself; help him to take more and more responsibility and help him manage gradually increasing freedom. The child should be studied as objectively as possible to know of what he is capable and when he is ready for new experiences and learning.

Parents tend to make the mistake of expecting too much of the child or not enough. Perhaps they do not realize when he is ready for wider freedom and responsibility, and therefore treat a four-year-old like a two-year-old. Parents need to plan—to have objectives, and to know how and what the child can learn, and to provide the opportunities for learning more when he is ready. Early in development the child needs to learn that living makes demands on him, and that there are requirements which must be met. He learns to accept these requirements when they are planned so that they are regular, consistent, reasonable and just.

Young children need wholesome patterns for imitation, for they imitate what they see and absorb what they hear. The attitudes, ideas, opinions, prejudices and ways of parents' behavior are copied by children.

Being a good parent requires constant study and learning. The good parent is a learner, open-minded and critical. He is also experimental in his attitude and approach to his problems as a parent. He takes advantage of the accumulating knowledge of child development, discusses with others the methods and techniques of training. He is observant, thoughtful and flexible. Above all, he wants his children to grow up—to advance toward the goal of maturity. Nothing can be more thrilling and satisfying than to watch and guide the development of a child. To see him becoming a happy, well-adjusted adult, taking his place in the world, meeting and dealing with his problems with courage and intelligence is the only reward a parent requires.

Why Parents Should Be Consistent

By RALPH K. MEISTER

WE HEAR a lot of talk about the best way of handling children. We read about it in magazines. We discuss it in groups and among ourselves. The only field of human endeavor that has more "systems" than the field of child guidance is probably betting on horse races. Concerning the latter, on which I am no expert, I shall say nothing. Concerning the former, however, I think it should be pointed out that no system, however excellent in theory, can work unless it has the active support of both parents. In fact, it seems to me that an appreciable number of children's problems in eating, sleeping, toilet training and discipline are made unnecessarily difficult because both parents haven't agreed on how they should be handled. Parenthetically, in case Grandmother or Grandfather should by some odd chance be reading this, the same adverse effects can be expected when there is not agreement between parents and grandparents, especially when all are living under the same roof.

The sooner there is fundamental agreement between the parents, the smoother will go the business of bringing up Baby. Mother believes that at bedtime, after the proverbial checks for an open diaper pin have been made and Baby is not teething or sick, the baby should be left alone until she falls asleep. Father, on the other hand, wants to go in every ten or fifteen minutes either to lecture or threaten or cajole. Naturally, we can expect both mother and child to have difficulty over the issue of going to bed. With the expectation of another visit from Daddy for the third and last time, wailing on a child's part is a very intelligent reaction. Certainly she should not be criticized for manifesting behavior which we indirectly encourage.

In the matter of self-help at mealtimes, Mother wants to let her fifteen-month-old son try out with fingers and spoon his skill in transporting food from plate to mouth. Father is made uncomfortable and tense by the resulting mess on Baby, high chair and floor. Some of this tension communicates itself to the child who may become clumsier and more awkward in performing this task under a disapproving eye.

Mother decides to let little eighteen-month-old Johnny who is still wetting during the day continue to do so until he establishes his own control by imitation (rather than persuasion or punishment) but Father, on the other hand, feels that his pride and joy should already be toilet trained like his cousin who is one month younger. Here we have a conflict between adults which cannot help but affect adversely the child's toilet training, whatever the method used. In all of these cases, it is best if parents agree on policy beforehand and then follow it consistently.

Two kinds of undesirable effects can be expected from a failure of parents to agree on issues of child care and training. In the first place, it will be more difficult for the child to learn what is expected of him in the same sense that children who have to learn two languages in the home do not have as fluent a command of language as children who have to learn to express themselves in only one language. Even more important, however, the learning will be more difficult for the child not only because it is more complicated but also because it has become charged with emotional tensions and disturbances. A child never "acts so dumb" as he does when he is anxious about parental approval or when he fears disapproval. We know how utterly stupid even an intelligent child can seem under these circumstances, and we must realize that some measure of disapproval of the child is always present when both parents do not agree. The child is frustrated because he has no consistent standard toward which he can strive.

In the second place, after the child has become confused and frustrated by parental inconsistency, he may somehow adjust to a bad situation but a new twist is added. As the child grows older, he learns to use the differences between parents to his own advantage. If Mother denies permission to go to the show, he may go and ask Father. More seriously, parental disagreements can become a competitive battleground for the child's affections to the disadvantage of all concerned. If one parent tends to be lenient and the other strict, or if the grandparents indulgently let Johnny disobey his mother's rules, then we are setting up a situation in which the child is going to be systematically robbed of the affection and companionship and example of one of his parents. Actually, such a situation means that one of the parents becomes the "saint" and the other parent becomes the "ogre." Then instead of getting a well-rounded affection from both parents, the child may tend to restrict himself to and to favor the more indulgent parent. The disapproval he feels from the less-favored parent is never completely erased and is not "made up" by the lavish overattention of the other parent. This kind of conflict should never arise if we parents take steps, from the very beginning and all along the way, to be sure that on the fundamentals we agree sufficiently to give our particular boy and girl the advantages of a consistent system of guidance at all stages in their development. The time we spend to achieve such a working agreement pays high dividends in happier children and fewer problems. It is part of our child's birthright.

LINCOLN

Lincoln was a very tall man, so tall that people who met him often remarked about his height. Once someone said to him, "You certainly have long legs, Mr. Lincoln." And Lincoln is reported to have answered, "They're only long enough to reach the ground."

—Ann King

"Read" Your Child — Behavior Speaks Volumes

By JAMES L. HYMES, JR.

H. Armstrong Roberts

Today books about child training are best-sellers. You have probably read several of them. You want to do a good job with your children and you welcome all the help you can get along the way.

This business of reading *about* children is a good idea. In the last twenty-five years a great deal has been found out — new facts about children's growth, new techniques for living happily with children, new insight into their inner world of feelings. Once we thought that children just grew. Now we know that certain conditions — attitudes, experiences, opportunities — help that growth. Children can develop with a maximum of comfort and ease, and with real happiness. They can grow to honest maturity. You want this for *your* youngsters and good books can help you achieve it.

But sometimes we rely on books too much. Perhaps this is a pitfall of modern times. Perhaps it is a particular pitfall for those of us who are most earnest and sincere with our children. And perhaps it is a very special danger for those of us who are well-educated. It is easy for us to come to believe that *all* of the truth is found in books, all wisdom, all good ideas. Our own long experience with schooling may build this error into us. It may even blind us to *other* ways of learning.

There are other ways. Your child can teach you, for example. You have to read *him* as well as read the books. You have to listen to his language and get meaning from it. It can teach you, along with the words from the printed page.

Children have a very special language. One important thing to know about it: they do not say everything in words. To get what they have to tell you you need to look and listen to *all* they do, to their total behavior: their expressions, gestures, the tension of their bodies; the look around their eyes; smiles, cries; the set of the mouth and the wrinkle of the nose. This is all language. It is the language of behavior. Learn to read it, along with your books.

This language of behavior is not "baby-talk." All of us, all humans of all ages, speak with our bodies. Our actions talk; our gestures have meaning. Think for a second of your own tight white knuckles when you are afraid; of the way you wet your lips when you are worried; of how you forget when you really don't want to do something; of your dancing eyes when something really tickles you. Behavior is a subtle language but it is a real one.

It is more than real, in fact. For often all people — but particularly children — use this language of behavior in a unique way. It can become our private language, our very special way of saying things with their most personal meaning — our way of saying those things that cut deepest with us — the feelings and reactions and wishes that are too precious to put into ordinary speech and words.

Once you are willing to tune yourself to it, this language is not hard to read. Smiles, relaxed bodies, whole-hearted interest, persistent seeking — these are some of the major words. Tears, worried looks, heads turned away, refusals—these, too, tell you.

The trick lies not in reading the language but in believing it. The signals come through clearly to you from your child. You will have no trouble getting them. But will you be willing to accept them as real language? Will you be able to bring yourself to act as if your child is telling you something fundamental?

Again, maybe the more you believe in books alone the harder it will be. But you can recognize this as a pitfall and guard yourself against it. You can get in tune if you want to.

Then the language is clear. Then there is little doubt as to the "right" thing to do. The language itself is so expressive that it tells you. You are on safe ground when things basically please your child; you are on shaky ground when he resists. If your child persistently goes after something; if all of his behavior adds up to his seeking it; if once he gets it every sign of body tells you he is glad, you can be pretty sure you are right. You may not know why. Your child may not know why. But when this wanting becomes so clear that body-language tells it to you, it is not just wanting, it is needing.

The opposite is also true. If it is something he basically avoids; if he fights against it, tenses as he deals with it; tightens up or evades it, you will know what to do . . . skip it if you can. You do not always have to know why. The "why" sometimes does not show until later. But take the language for what it says.

What do you read? Books certainly, and articles and columns . . . as much as you can. But read your child too. Let the language of his behavior also tell you. It can give you leads, cues, hints, hunches that let you soften the edges and build the warm relationships you want, that let you ease the strains of growing up and build for a future on a stable, comfortable base.

For Father

When we pay tribute to our fathers, we not only honor the head of our own immediate household with the love and praise that is his due; we are also dedicating our thankful respect to all the great men of history, our forefathers, who left to us the heritage of a life worth living.
—Esther Baldwin York

Edward Lettau

Why Parents Say "No"

By LESTER A. KIRKENDALL

I STOPPED MY CAR at a filling station for gasoline. As the station attendant was filling the tank, his wife and their young daughter drove up. The girl leaned out the car window and asked eagerly, "Dad, may I...?" The last words of the request were lost in the roar of a passing truck. As the truck rolled on, Dad raised his head and replied, "No."

The girl was deeply disappointed. Tears were close when Mother interceded with, "Why, John, don't you think it would be all right for her to go?"

John looked a bit bewildered and asked, "What did she want?"

Suddenly I realized that it isn't only children who say *No* to almost any suggestion. Why should saying *No* become such a habit that a parent says it automatically? The follow-ing reasons for the "no-habit" have emerged from discussions with parents:

1. *They say No in self-defense— too many requests might "drive them to distraction."* While parents may think their *No's* a protection, the continual stream of *May I's* also has its meaning. It is a reflection of the child's dependence upon his parents. For the very young child there are few activities in which he can engage without parents' permission. But, as the child grows older, new situations and new desires arise and the requests grow even more frequent and persistent.

2. *They feel they must protect their children.* This is a sound enough reason. There are times when the child has to be protected with a *No* or a definite limitation, yet the same suggestion of an appraisal holds here.

27

Very frequently the child seeks to do things which may result in immediate and obvious physical dangers of one kind or another. While seeking to avoid these dangers, parents may forget the more distant and less obvious psychological dangers which may result from overprotection: making the child unduly fearful, producing isolation by excluding him from activities of his group, or limiting his chance to grow in resourcefulness and independence.

Parents often think of their task as one of protection. However, it might be more accurate to say their real task is one of weighing immediate against long-run consequences, the psychological against the physical (and these cannot be fully separated), and risks to be run against values to be gained.

The next two reasons for saying *No* usually are unvoiced and unrecognized.

3. *They carry over resentment from their own childhood experiences.* It is hard for parents to realize they may be refusing requests their children make because they, as children, were refused similar privileges and were resentful over the refusal. I often find such resentments expressed in my college classes in family relations. Sometimes I ask students who have younger brothers or sisters if they have ever felt a younger sibling "was getting away with murder" —that they would like to have the chance to straighten him out. The proportion who have felt, or still feel, that way is large. Before these young people become parents, they need to talk out such resentments or they may find themselves saying *No* without real reason.

4. *They need to demonstrate their authority.* Many students in family relations classes remember instances in which the usual childish *Why* to a parental *No* was answered with the reply, "Just because I said *No.*"

One of the students commented, "By golly, that was the reason, too." This need for authority sometimes arises from a sense of insecurity and uncertainty on the part of parents. They may fear that children will begin to take advantage unless constantly checked. They may feel that an obvious exercise of authority produces respect.

5. *They unconsciously fall into a negative frame of mind.* One mother found herself in this situation when her five-year-old son came to her with a request which he ended with, "I can't do it, can I Mother?"

The mother said, "I suddenly realized he felt he would be refused permission on any request he made." Her reaction was to formulate some principles for dealing with her children. They were:

1. Listen to the child's request and try to evaluate it objectively.

2. Say *No* only when real danger or a problem of convenience for others is involved.

3. Analyze her own reasons for saying *No.*

Parents and children form images of each other and of themselves. Parents' images seldom keep pace with the actual growth of their child. The result is that they often see the child as a less mature individual than do his teachers or other parents in the neighborhood. Many a parent has been surprised to hear someone outside the family comment favorably on the maturity of his child.

Children often regress in behavior when they are around their parents. I once remarked to my teen-age daughter that I thought children fall back about two years when they enter their own homes. She agreed.

28

Do You Compete for Affection?

By RALPH K. MEISTER

"BUT MOTHER SAID I could!" or "Daddy said it was o.k. with him." How many parents have heard these words as clinching arguments from little Junior or Mary when ordinary pleas failed? Or perhaps these words may have introduced a particular request—in which case, they only thinly veiled the mildly threatening question "Now you're not going to be so cruel or heartless as to deny me this, are you?"

What *is* going on here? Of course it is evident that there is some inconsistency in what Father and Mother said if Junior is reporting accurately. Junior may not be innocent in his playing of one parent against the other and, if so, discipline is likely to suffer. Ordinarily we can clear up such misunderstanding and confusion by having a general rule to the effect that the first opinion holds; whether Father or Mother expressed it, the child must not carry a denied plea to another court. However, if this happens frequently in your family, it may indicate beginnings of a problem.

Shortly after the baby comes from the hospital there is some good-natured competition about whom he'll smile at first or later on, whether he'll learn to say "Dada" first or "Mama" first. It is a rare parent who does not wish for and seek some emotional response from the child. Actually this is legitimate and is one of the joys of parenthood. We want our children to love us and to show us they are aware of us as individuals who are important to them. However, in the course of growing up, a child at one time will favor one parent somewhat over the other and, at another time, reverse his preference. Junior at two may cling to Mother in a manner that makes Father doubt whether he counts for much but, at six, Junior may think there is no person so wonderful as his Dad. At twelve Mary may feel her Father is God's gift to all womankind, whereas at six the sun rose and set in Mother. These are extreme examples but they serve to illustrate the changing preferences of a growing child. Like the political party that is out of office, the parent in second position has consolation that his or her day will come. The best state of affairs is where preference for one parent is not too extreme, and where there is a mutual flow of affection between the child and both parents.

If we encounter a situation where the child competitively pits one parent against the other—to see which will allow him most privileges or be the most lenient—it's time to take inventory of our attitudes to see if we are contributing unwittingly to this state of affairs. Very often conflict between parents is the fertile soil in which such seeds of discord germinate. A mother, unhappy with her husband, may find solace in showering affection and attention on her son, unconsciously alienating him from his father. Or a father, finding he's not as effective as he'd like to be, may seek to be compensated in the adoring eyes of a daughter whom he indulges. Competition between parents for the affection of the child —a kind of helpless pawn—is damaging to the child's personality development; it causes conflict and guilt about the apparent neglect of the less-preferred parent. Even in much milder cases where competition between parents is less intense and does not result from a serious rift, such competition can destroy the good discipline, respect and affection each parent deserves from his children.

We cannot deny likelihood and value of individuality and uniqueness in the child's relation to his parents. A boy feels different toward his mother than he does toward his father—a girl, likewise. However, the child derives his greatest sense of security in knowing he is loved by both parents and that he doesn't have to choose between them. A question from the gallery? Yes, you're quite right; I would not recommend parents *ever* asking their child—even in jest—whether he likes Mommy best or Daddy best. We may be kidding or doing it for amusement "to see what Junior will say," but emotionally it is not "good business."

Two parents to love and to be loved. That's the best arrangement.

Be Yourself

By ANGELO PATRI

Honora recently had come to America from Ireland . . . Her cheeks were like rosy apples, her hair unmistakably red, her accent charming Irish. A friendly child, she went to the playground only to have other children tease her. "Irish, Irish, red-headed Irish," they chanted.

Shocked by unfriendliness, suddenly fearful, Honora ran home crying. "What's this? They called you Irish? And red-headed? Aren't you Irish?" asked her mother.

"Yes, but—"

"Never mind the but. You're Irish and you're red-headed. Nobody called you an untrue name so back you go and let those children know you're not ashamed of your father and mother or your ancestors . . ." With that, the mother washed Honora's face, brushed her hair and, with a loving pat, sent her back to the playground where she earned respect . . .

Every American citizen is entitled to acceptance, respect and consideration of his fellows. Every one of us has his roots in another land. Each family contributes to the strength and the wealth of this nation . . . Our laws, religions, institutions sprang from those of another time, another land. They are contributions from peoples whose histories are proud and honorable.

Let us teach our children to respect their father's language, religion and history and thus enable them to build a rich heritage for their children. The strength, intelligence and courage that go into the making of a fine American citizen are built on stout self-respect. Hopes for brotherhood and unity rest with our children.

From an article written in the interest of Brotherhood Week, sponsored by the National Conference of Christians and Jews.

The Glad Gift of Laughter

By LUCY NULTON

"I call this Fun House." Fern laughed and took a big bite.

"I don't," responded Doris. "I call it Gingerbread House because we come here to play with Ruthie an' we eat gingerbread an' laugh."

"I call it Home," said Ruthie quietly.

For the young child who is healthily living in a happy home surrounded by love, mere being is exuberance. His well-being bubbles over in gurgles, crows, chuckles and play. He breathes in the atmosphere of cheerfulness—Mother singing at her work, Father whistling as he putters —assimiliates it and makes it part of his growth. In every child, as well as in every adult, there is deep need for laughter just for laughter's sake.

Along with singing, whistling, joking at our work, we may fill his need first with the play of the bath— happy chatter, making a play of the undressing, patting, sloshing, drying: singing and chanting fun rhythms, phrases, rhymes, and even great and profound adult poetry which carries in it rhythm and word music.

Then there are toe plays and finger plays, exquisite delight as each little digit is waggled rhythmically or caressed with a chant. (No child who has had this play from infancy can be completely without concept of the number ten when he starts to school.) Sheer joyous sensation bubbles over in laughter, rhythm, grace, as the young child responds to his mother's joy and the relaxation of these plays.

Mother Goose rhymes and nursery rhymes come next, for adult though they were in composition. they are filled with elements which make humor for the young child: the unexpected, the grotesque quality of falling (particularly delighting if it is a grownup falling); the impossibility of a cow jumping over the moon, of riding the skies in a basket. the sea in a tub; the sublimation of a fear in being able to laugh at Miss Muffet; the natural, inborn satisfaction of play with vocal sounds and nonsense syllables; the amazing fun of things topsy-turvy; the delighted assurance of finding these rhymes always the same. "Say it again. Say it again. Say it again!" Here is fun!

Riddles follow rhymes. Exaggerations—so much fun in physical play for the very young—now find words and becomes jokes or tall tales. As he grows old enough to have an assured background of knowledge and words, his sense of humor rolics through collections of riddles and after them, puns. At first they are confused, pointless, interminable. Finally they emerge in the nine- and ten-year-old in clever, original jokes, puns, yarns. First jokes—at four, five, six, seven years—need understanding, patience, insight from adults. They seldom thrive on corrections. They never thrive when the adult laughs at the child instead of at the joke. A joke shared is enhanced, but a joke stared at goes flat.

Pat-a-Cake, Pat-a-Cake—

At many periods he chortles over nonsense syllables and tongue twisters, such as one of Eugene Field's poems, Edward Lear's "Nonsense Rhymes," and the alliterative difficulties of folklore tongue twisters.

While he is still very young, it takes so little to make a joke: exaggerated posturing, giant steps, sing-songs, new words chanted into unaware vocabulary growth, different tones of voice (whispering, deep, shrill). To us who have grown so far away from sheer nonsense, exaggeration and incongruity, they often may seem silly. But here is relaxation which may be shared by adults as nonsensical relief in an expanding, wondrous, adventurous, but burden-heavy era. Perhaps this so-called nonsense is not so nonsensical after all.

For the very young, sensations are funny: the slithering of sand through the fingers, squishing of mud between the toes. These are laughter to one who perceives their delightfulness.

So, too, is light teasing when relationships are warm—a wee pinch off the mud pie, a tweaked toe through the sand pile, a waggling of fingers against fingers when exploring a tunnel. These are the early communications of teasing fun and relaxing laughter.

From six months to a long time after, the fun of the unexpected, the exaggerated, the upside-down, is found in bumps, tumbles, "peep-eye," peek-a-boo, later in hide-and-seek. At four, five, six, seven, "Boo!" is exquisitely funny, particularly if the grownup startles easily and exaggeratedly.

Running is fun. Joy comes in such moments. Accomplishment is accompanied by skipping, singing or chanting. Sometimes the young child sings his thoughts like a psalm.

There is much in the life of the child which has no purpose — as adults see purpose. Life is lived for the moment—an ecstasy, clear, full of sensation, priceless. When we may, without intruding or clumsily shattering, we share these moments with him—if we still have the heart of a child.

Scarcely any heritage is comparable to that of having deeply seeded into one's childhood the joys, companionship and ecstacies of a happy family group having fun together. The inheritance is complete when, at times, that group can expand, taking in one's friends to make them part of the belonging.

Laughing all together *with* each other—never *at* another until the child is maturely ready to start the laughing at himself—we explore, adventure, laugh, play. Deliberately seeking light-heartedness, serenity, steady realism, we endow him as we can with a shield of laughter—gay laughter, kind and loving.

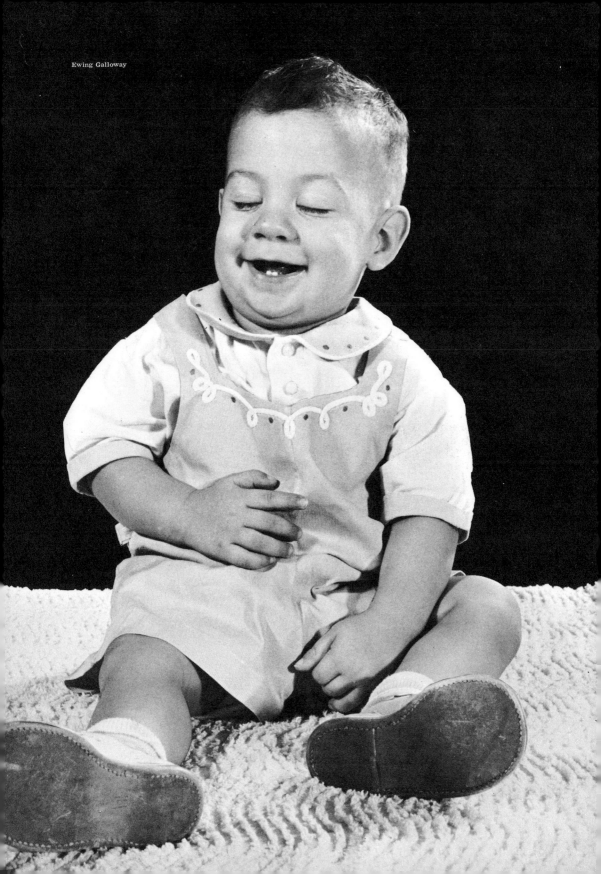

The New Neighborhood

By ELIZABETH MECHEM FULLER

Families move about so much these days. Whenever parents and children move into a new neighborhood, many problems, some real and some imaginary, must be faced. Even adults experienced in social relations find it hard to meet new neighbors and to settle into "life-as-usual" routines in a few hours. Things are not made any easier when young Karen or "Butch" tearfully describe how badly the neighborhood children are treating them. Nor does it help for the new family to sit back and pout or to be haughty and defensive. Rightfully or not, it usually falls upon the newcomers to carry the major responsibility for their adjustment and acceptance.

Edward Lettau

When moving into a new neighborhood, everyone likes to make a good impression, but not everyone knows how to make one easily and quickly. For one thing, there is a tendency for the "new" family to dress up too much. How often we see a new child at play in immaculate and "too good" clothing! She looks very nice—oh yes —but what is the effect she really makes? She is *different* rather than *like* the others, a fatal mistake so far as her quick and easy acceptance by the other children is concerned.

Then there is the impressive (to the adult, at least) toy. Give unfamiliar Tommy a unique or expensive toy to introduce in the neighborhood, and in spite of good intentions to the contrary, Tommy either seems more different or he is "taken in" not for himself but for his toy. Tommy cannot maintain this kind of acceptance unless he keeps on contributing bigger and better toys, literally buying his friendships. Once, seven-year-old Tommy, new to his group, hopefully took a brand new Jet-Jumper (pogo stick with spring action) out-of-doors right after Christmas, expecting all of the boys and girls to gather 'round for turns. After a few curious looks and cautious trials the children left the shovelled walk for their backyard snow fort which was a group project, and there stood Tommy with his Jet Jumper—still outside the group. How much better it would have been for Tommy's mother to help Tommy find an old piece of pipe or pasteboard tubing to contribute for a snow fort chimney! Strategy — that's what it takes — not expensive trappings!

Mother, too, can take a tip from the behavior of the neighborhood youngsters toward the new child. Sleek lounging pajamas and gold mules may have their dramatic effect under the proper conditions, but rarely do they speed a young housewife's acceptance among a group of neighborhood wives where the usual workaday garb is blue jeans and T-shirt or cotton housedress.

Paradoxically the best way to make an impression in most neighborhoods is to avoid being impressive. There are some who might feel that such advice is a plea for conformity or mediocrity. Not at all—once "in," things are different. However, initial conformity is such an ingrained part of our culture that a rather "folksy" approach works best—revelation of talent, possessions, or uniqueness is taken in stride later on. The flexible, well-adjusted person—either child or adult—recognizes and accepts temporary sacrifices of individuality in order to encourage group "belongingness."

Occasionally real cultural differences prevail in neighborhoods, particularly in cities and towns where outlying areas housed but a few families until new subdivisions were developed and young people with small children began to move in. In one such neighborhood, three families of foreign birth who had lived there about ten years became completely surrounded by young and modern suburbanites. At first there was no exchange of friendship at all, nothing but mutual withdrawal, scoldings for the newcomers' children, and taunts for the broken English spoken by the older residents. Then one day Marge Kirkpatrick, one of the young mothers, volunteered to canvas her neighborhood for the Red Cross fund —on her list was old Mrs. Polvik, the most resistant of all of the original home-owners. Though she had dreaded going there, when Mrs. Polvik opened her door, Marge was so overcome by the beauty of the hand-embroidered jacket and slippers she wore that she could not even say

"Red Cross." After an hour's visit during which she had ordered a similar jacket for herself, had admired several beautiful oil paintings, and had eaten some pastry the like of which she had never before tasted, Marge had this to say, *It just makes me ill to think we have lived here for six whole months without knowing that woman!* The upshot of it is that Mrs. Polvik uses her sewing scraps to make caps, belts, scarfs, and mukluks for neighborhood children and the children shovel her walks and mow her lawn.

Mrs. Povlik introduced the other two families, who turned out to have in their repertoires (over and above being delightful people) —two of the most reliable baby-sitters in the area; a son who could teach piano; a wonderful collection of pictures of their native lands, a mother who made delicious bread and cakes at very low cost, and—imagine this—a jeep with a snowplow attachment that solved the winter driveway problem for everyone in the area! The real problem was not the earlier residents in the neighborhood, but for the newcomers to find enough assets to bargain *with* and to be friendly *with*. It works both ways, of course. Not all neighbors, it is true, are such glamorous people as the Polviks and their friends, but that, too, is as it should be because the vast majority of us have rather prosaic needs and want only to sit and chat with other ordinary people.

The present outlook is for our society to have to face much shifting from one place to another for military, business, housing, or other reasons. The resultant neighborhoods face most of the problems of a "United Nations" organization in miniature.

II

Your Child Deserves Unconditional Love

By BLAINE M. PORTER

THERE ARE FEW EXPERIENCES, if any, that surpass parenthood in responsibilities which go along with it, or in satisfactions that result from it. The anticipation of having children begins in the lives of many individuals long before they marry. As the time nears for children to arrive in the family, expectant parents imagine or dream even more specifically of what their child will be like or how they hope he will be. This is illustrated in a conversation I had not long ago with a friend who was expecting a baby soon. She said, "I'm so excited! I can hardly wait until my baby is born. If it's a girl I'm going to have so much fun dressing her up in cute little dresses and fixing her hair. We'll go lots of places and do interesting things. And as she grows up she is going to be a real little lady and know how to behave properly. She isn't going to be a tomboy like some girls I've seen. I'll teach her the manners and graces she needs to know in order to

Edward Lettau

be welcomed company in the best of groups. We'll be companions, and I'll love her and she'll love me.

"If it's a boy, I want him to be all boy! I'll teach him to kick a football, to hit a baseball, and I'll buy him an electric train. We'll pretend we're cowboys and Indians, firemen and trainmen, and share many other experiences. I'll teach him to be polite and courteous, in a man's way—I don't want him to be a sissy. We'll share ideas and secrets and he'll love me and I'll love him. So you see, it doesn't matter whether I have a boy or a girl. It will be wonderful in either case."

It always is a pleasure to see someone as excited and thrilled over the anticipated arrival of a baby as was my friend. The other day when I received an announcement of the birth of her daughter, I found myself reflecting upon what she had said. "I'll love her and she'll love me." That's fine, of course. But somehow those words seemed clouded with her other statements. "And as she grows up she is going to be a real little lady and know how to behave properly. She isn't going to be a tomboy like some girls I've seen." If she is a normal child, there undoubtedly will be times when she is not going to fit into this preconceived dream of a little girl who always behaves properly. Before she becomes a lady she must be a little girl, and while being a little girl she may not always be a "little lady." There will be times when her child will be tired, angry or unhappy when quite likely she will "misbehave" and, regardless of how normal the behavior might be, it will not fit into this mother's conception of "proper behavior." And what if her daughter sometimes does show signs of being a tomboy? This would be neither unusual nor abnormal. I wonder if this mother's love will be determined by her child's behavior? This is an important question, especially if the child's behavior does not meet the expectations of her mother.

Parents (well, *most* parents) from the beginning of recorded history have professed to love their children. However, if it were possible to probe into the minds and thinking of a group of parents, we would find that the word "love" means different things to different individuals. We would also be likely to find that the way love is expressed varies considerably from one individual to another. And if we also inquired about the motives behind the love, we would discover that different parents "love" their children for different reasons.

We do not have to agree upon the same definition of love. Neither do we have to express it in the same way, nor possess the same motives. But if we include in our concept of love a feeling of affection for the child, and a desire to nurture and to care for him, then it is important that the love be given freely, without attached strings. It is important, too, that it be given in an unselfish way, and not for the primary purpose of serving adult needs. It should be given unconditionally.

Johnny had been practicing every spare moment in the hope that he would be able to get the shortstop position on his school's baseball team. When the line-up was announced and he wasn't even selected as a substitute, he was crushed. As he told the news to his family at dinner that evening,

his father responded: "Well, you should have known you couldn't compete with all those other kids when you can't catch a ball any better than you can. If you had spent your time earning some money like I told you to instead of wasting all that time practicing, see how much better off you would be now."

If Johnny had won the shortstop position and, by chance, had turned out to be the hero of some game, it is quite likely that this father would have been there collecting the laurels and sharing the honors. Johnny needed support and love in a period of great disappointment. This could have been an opportunity for the father to prove to Johnny that he loved him whether he succeeded or failed.

There are many times in the life of an individual when he experiences failure. These may include learning to eat, learning to share, learning to control elimination, learning to ride a tricycle, and so on. Disappointment may range from a balloon bursting in the hands of a two-year-old, a ten-year-old losing his favorite pocketknife, to a 17-year-old failing to get the lead in the school play. It is important to them to have your support at these times of disappointment or failure. I'm not suggesting that one must replace the balloon or pocketknife, or try to bribe the coach into letting your son play on the team, or intercede with the drama director in order to get the lead part for your daughter. I am saying, let them know you love them just as much, whether they win or lose, succeed or fail. *The first characteristic of a parent who loves his child unconditionally is that he offers support and love at all times —shares his child's joys and sorrows, supports him in failures as well as successes.*

Habits Can Be a "Thing"

By JAMES L. HYMES, JR.

Edward Lettau

Parenthood is not an easy job, and one reason is that you have to learn to treat CHILDREN differently from the way you handle THINGS.

You make a THING by setting up a pattern and sticking to it. Once it is established, success follows automatically. This is THING-PSYCHOLOGY—no mistakes—no deviations—no changes. But HUMAN PSYCHOLOGY is different. People—children—grow and develop. Unless we get that difference clearly in our minds, we will keep applying a thing-psychology to our youngsters, thus cheating ourselves out of the fun of a happy family life.

If you use a thing (habit)—psychology with children, you have to stand on constant guard to make sure that nothing ever goes wrong, to pick them up on every mistake, no matter how small. This psychology applied to children can bring changes in YOU that you will not like. You have to keep high standards, strive for perfection, and push all the time to get the super-best out of the children.

Some parents want their infants to be dry at the first moment possible; to be weaned at the earliest moment. Crawling isn't good enough; walking must come quickly. Babbling is a waste of time; talking one-two-three is all that matters.

The fear of "bad habits" is largely just imaginary. When the bladder muscles grow enough, children stay dry. When their eye muscles grow enough, they will read. Keep this in mind too, children do not grow in a straight line. The day by day trend is toward better behavior, but there are ups and downs. Don't worry about all the downs. Two-year-olds say "no;" four-year-olds sometimes say bad words. They act this way but get over it. Children are not things, they grow.

This is not to say that you never correct or discipline a child. All parents and teachers have to. The more you use a thing-psychology, the more you find that you nag and correct, and there is something much more important for parents to do. Enjoy children. Draw the line between *people* and *things*. Develop a NEW "common sense" about children and have much more good living with your youngsters.

38

Preparation for Marriage Begins at Birth

By LESTER A. KIRKENDALL

Preparation for marriage begins at birth. It begins with the attitudes and feelings which are built in the infant and small child toward sex roles, men-women relationships, sex, his own feeling of worth and adequacy as a boy or a girl, and similar matters.

Attitudes toward sex roles provide a good example. Over and over again one sees that the adult's concept of how he should behave as man or woman has an important bearing on his marriage adjustment. Especially is this true when the self-concepts of the husband and wife are in conflict or when one's individual concepts conflict with the role his mate expects him to play. When the wife, for example, feels the husband should take an active and interested part in caring for their infant but he feels it is the woman's place, or the husband feels he should but is not permitted to there is likely to be unhappiness if not conflict.

Ideas about proper roles are built through observations made by the child, what he hears and experiences. Family living is a forceful source of instruction. Parents can help their children toward an easier marital adjustment or increase their chances for difficulty by what they say and the way they live in the home.

Rigid, inflexible concepts of what a man or woman does are more likely to cause difficulty than a feeling that traditional sex lines can be crossed. "A man always handles the money." "A woman's place is in the home." "Only a sissy would work in the kitchen." Such rigid concepts when carried into adult life leave the individual incapable of quick, flexible adaptability.

Parents teach for this inflexibility by sharply limiting the roles within which their children can perform to their satisfaction. Girls who want to play with typical boys' toys, or little boys who play with dolls may be told that members of their sex "do not behave that way."

Along with this teaching goes the implication that the parent disapproves or is disappointed with this crossing of sex lines. This is much more often the case with boys than girls. For example, a girl may play with a football with more approval than a boy with a doll. It is more permissible for a girl to be rough and loud, than for a boy to be affectionate, yielding, or quiet. We often see boys or young men who are fearful of being thought unmanly if they express interest in an infant, indicate a desire for affection, or display some typical feminine interest.

There is more chance of difficulty in later adjustment if the child's pride in his sex is built at the expense of the other. A father in attempting to teach his son to handle tools said, "Son, you hold a hammer like a woman," and "you saw like a girl." His tone of voice left no doubt but that he thought very poorly of women's capacities, and that he was disappointed with his son's efforts. What he taught was a contempt for women, and when the boy was unable to handle the tools to his father's satisfaction, a distaste for the effort which caused the boy to abandon it.

There are many clichés used by members of both sexes about the other which lead children to feel a disrespect or contempt for those who behave so. "A man always has the easiest row to hoe." "You can never depend on a woman driver." "Women have no financial sense." "Women always get their way by crying." Such statements are not only false but they create feelings and resentments which prevent the sexes from working cooperatively. Also members of each sex may accept these appraisals of themselves as true and accurate and try to live up to them.

What do parents need to do to give their children concepts of sex roles which will better fit them for marriage?

They need to challenge their preconceptions (and often misconceptions) as to what is proper or acceptable behavior for men and women. Concepts in which members of one sex attain status through a particular pattern of work are dangerous. A child needs to see his father occasionally helping with the dishes or with the washing and his mother sometimes wielding a hammer or helping to mow the lawn.

Men and women need to be proud of their sex membership. They need to feel they have achieved their status through worthwhile achievements of their own rather than that they are superior because the other sex is so inferior.

Parents need to accept their child as an individual with unique capacities, interests, and potentialities, rather than as a boy or a girl. One too often sees fathers who wanted a son but got a daughter. Such men usually hold rigid concepts of sex roles to begin with. Their disappointment then leads them to try to build the daughter's patterns of interest and behavior along masculine lines. They will want her to play ball or fish with them but reject a game of dolls with her. The result is that the daughter often realizes her sex is rejected and in an effort to gain the approval of her father rejects her sex herself. She then may become a woman who has difficulty adjusting to marriage because in a measure she has rejected herself as a woman.

Men and women are different, of course, and so there always will and should be sex roles. But if they were more flexible, appreciative, and consciously thought through, the preparation of children for marriage would be better.

On Being a Child

Do you know what it is to be a child? It is to be something very different from the man of today . . . It is to believe in loveliness, to believe in belief; it is to be so little that the elves can reach to whisper in your ear; it is to turn pumpkins into coaches, and mice into horses; lowness into loftiness, and nothing into everything, for each child has a fairy godmother in its soul.

—FRANCES THOMPSON
(From Clifton's "Food for Thot")

"Though we travel the world over to find the beautiful, we must carry it with us or we find it not."

—RALPH WALDO EMERSON

Baby Sitters

By MARTHA B. RANSOHOFF

Where are all the women who used to be available to help the young mother—Grandma, Aunt Mary, or even a friendly neighbor? Today they have other interests, and if Mother is ill or has to go on an errand, she has to get a baby sitter.

Some children are friendly and do not mind strange people coming into their homes, while others are decidedly uncomfortable in the presence of a new person in the household. It is better, though, for someone to come in than to leave them with a neighbor or even Grandma. Children feel more secure in their own environment. They like to be surrounded by familiar objects; they know where their toys are, they are used to sleeping in their own beds, and eating at their own table.

Before the mother leaves, she should outline the children's routine, exactly what they are to do, the approximate time they are to go to bed, whether they may eat between meals, what they eat at mealtime, etc. The mother should also give the sitter a list of telephone numbers stating where the parents, some responsible person, or the pediatrician may be reached in case some question arises.

Children like people who know their ways, and it is ideal if the baby sitter can come to visit while Mother is at home and then come back at a future date when Mother has to go out on an errand. In a visit a baby sitter can learn the children's habits. All eating, sleeping and bathroom habits can be handled more smoothly if the baby sitter knows what to expect of the children and what special words they use to express their desires.

If the baby sitter learns to know the individual child and the household routine, many problems of baby sitting may be avoided. Parents will find happier and more contented children when they return home, the baby sitter won't be so exhausted when she leaves her job. In fact, she may even look forward to returning.

When left with a sitter, the child should always be assured that the parents will return. Parents can be specific and say they will be back for a certain meal or when the child wakes up.

The sitter should also be told what she is allowed to do, what she may eat, whether she may use the telephone, the record player, radio or television.

When there are several children in the family, it is probable that some friction will arise sometime during the sitter's stay. The two-year-old may try to demand attention while the baby is being fed. The sitter should anticipate this difficulty by giving the two-year-old some toys and a place to play before she starts to feed the baby. Even a six-year-old may demand attention but a child this age can also be diverted if something interesting is planned.

These suggestions are not only for young baby sitters, but are also for relatives, even Grandma and Grandpa, and friends who are eager to help the young Mother with her children. All need to learn the parents' way of doing things.

What Would You Do About
TANTRUMS?

By RALPH K. MEISTER

BABY ANNETTE, ten months old, has been confined by Mother to her play pen. She objects strenuously, shaking at the bars until she finally falls, kicking and yelling in a regular tantrum.

What would you do?

(a) Ignore Annette completely, going about your business.

(b) Return to her and give her one firm swift slap on her bottom to indicate that such behavior is not approved.

(c) Scold her, showing by your expression and tone of voice that you, too, are angry—at least as angry as she is.

(d) Take her out of the play pen and comfort her, perhaps playing with her for a little while, after which you return her to the play pen once more.

(e) Remain calm, cool and collected, giving her some toys or a cookie to divert her.

Discussion

Temper tantrums in children this young usually are the child's natural and normal response to a frustrating situation. They should not be considered misbehavior since the child at this age can neither conceal his true feelings nor is he socialized enough to know they are unacceptable. Therefore, both alternatives (b) and (c) are out; (c) is especially poor procedure since it subjects the child to a strong rejecting emotional response on our part. (d) seems unfeasible: Such a reaction may encourage the child to temper displays to command or coerce our attention and affection, which is a poor basis for giving. (e) would be the recommended alternative, with especial emphasis upon our remaining calm. Nothing quenches anger in quite such short order as not having it reinforced by an adult's getting angry in return.

Alternative (a)? For certain parents and children, (a) occasionally works. However it is not recommended here because, for most parents, this results in their getting steamed up—they are likely to have what should have been alternative (a) abruptly turned into alternative (b). Parents, too, have their weaknesses.

What Would You Do About
TOILET TRAINING?

By RALPH K. MEISTER

Betty continues to wet the bed and to soil her clothes in spite of having had toilet training for several months. She even objects to periodic seatings throughout the day even though she will often wet immediately after being re-diapered.

If you were Betty's parents, what would YOU do?

a. Administer a mild spanking on those occasions where there is wetting or soiling right after being re-diapered.

b. Discontinue toilet training for a month or two and meanwhile re-diaper when necessary without fussing or blaming or scolding the child.

c. Let the child ask to be seated and praise her when she is successful.

d. Show strong verbal disapproval of wetting.

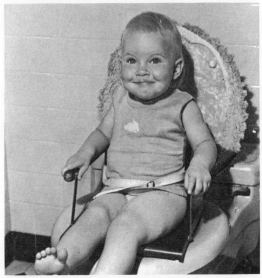

Constance Bannister

e. Refuse to change soiled or wet diapers oftener than twice or three times a day until sufficient control is established.

Discussion

"A" and "D" are the poorest methods because they tend to create a highly emotional resistive attitude toward the problem. They may disturb the child so much as to make training almost impossible. "E" may have the same effect if the child objects to a wet or soiled diaper or "E" may get him so accustomed to this condition that he has less personal incentive to remain dry. "B" would probably be the necessary first step to allow the emotional tension over the issue to subside. Thereafter policy "C" might be instituted. When the child is not forced but is made partially responsible and receives recognition for his efforts, training should progress normally.

What Would You Do About
CRYING AT NAPTIME?

By RALPH K. MEISTER

Lynn, age 18 months, after taking her nap alone for months, now cries when mother leaves the room.

If you were Lynn's parents, what would YOU do?

a. Leave the room without one backward glance and let Lynn cry it out.

b. Pick her up and rock her until she falls asleep again.

c. Dispense with her nap.

d. Sit by her crib until she is asleep.

e. Keep her up until she is too sleepy to resist a nap.

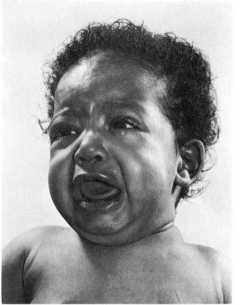

H. Armstrong Roberts

Discussion

Lynn still needs to have an afternoon nap so (c) would be inappropriate. Though she should not be put to bed for a nap too early, (e) is inappropriate because if the child is allowed to get too tired she will become fretful and make falling asleep less likely. (b) may work but placing her in her crib may reawaken her. This may lead to an undesirable state of affairs where Lynn has to be rocked many times for one nap and she may get enough rest during the rockings so that she will not want and probably will not need her nap. (d) is probably most appropriate. The child at this age is becoming socialized to an extent where she is dependent upon her mother's presence for the complete relaxation that allows her to go to sleep. As she gets older she will outgrow this particular dependence but at this stage of her development such time spent with her is a good investment. (a) usually makes going to bed a battle which not only is a strain on both mother and child, but may postpone ultimately falling asleep. Meeting the child half way in her sleep requirements is usually the best policy in the long run.

What Would You Do About
HELPING FATHER DRIVE?

By RALPH K. MEISTER

Father, mother, and Edward, age eighteen months, are out for a Sunday drive. Edward insists on "helping father drive" by holding on to the steering wheel. This is obviously unsafe procedure.

If you were Edward's parents, what would YOU do?

(a) Have mother and Edward sit in the back seat.

(b) Pull Edward away from the wheel every time he reaches for it.

(c) Slap Edward smartly on the hands with an accompanying "no, no" when he tries to hold the wheel.

(d) Pull off to the side of the road and give Edward his fill of toying with the wheel. When he is bored, continue.

(e) Pick a side street or side road and let Edward steer sitting in father's lap in return for letting the wheel alone when driving on the highway.

Discussion

Only if mother likes wrestling as a part of Sunday's drive would we use alternative (b). Most mothers find such a procedure rather exhausting. (d) may eventually bore Edward but the odds are that you will be bored much sooner; therefore (d) is impractical. So is (e). Edward isn't old enough to know enough to abide by such a bargain. Further, it is likely to make this particular form of nuisance even more attractive for Edward. (c) is the preferred alternative, not only for the present moment but to settle the matter for the future. Letting a child play in this manner is dangerous. If we might be willing to risk Edward's neck and our own, we should still consider the other innocent people with whom we must share the highway. If we cannot bring ourselves to educate Edward to the prohibition as in (c), then alternative (a) combined with some distraction can be used. However, it is a very temporary kind of solution. The next time he sits in the front seat, in all likelihood Edward will show the same behavior.

What Would You Do About
A LITTLE GIRL OUT LATE?

By RALPH K. MEISTER

Edward Lettau

Karen has been out late with her parents, visiting her grandparents. Now she is peevish and objects to being undressed and going to bed.

If you were Karen's parents, what would YOU do?

(a) Facilitate things by playing with Karen so as to amuse her and distract her attention from present discomforts.

(b) Hold her in your arms and rock her for a while to calm her down.

(c) Proceed with as much dispatch as possible to get Karen ready for bed and into bed without delay.

(d) Give Karen a mild slap to make her "straighten out."

(e) Get home early.

Discussion

Children in need of sleep can usually be expected to act "bratty." They are too tired to be pleasant, much less reasonable. Therefore, the best policy is to accept their peevishness and get them to bed in the shortest time possible, alternative (c). It will save their temper and yours. Alternative (a) seems more likely to prolong the upset, (b) to postpone the real solution. (d) isn't at all fair to Karen. Alternative (e)? This is the alternative that will have its strong appeal to bachelor uncles and maiden aunts, unversed in the complexities of visiting with children. Of course, if you can do it, fine! But it is not always possible or feasible.

Young Children's Eagerness To Learn

III

By MARGUERITA RUDOLPH

It is a common sight these days to see young fathers attending to shopping in the company of a young child. This is often a great adventure to the child who is so eager for knowledge.

A boy of about four was tugging at his father's coat in a big store. *"Daddy, daddy, what's that?"* The child was pointing his finger to an intricate bright metal fixture. The father paid no attention and continued business-like with his shopping. *"Daddy, what's that red thing on the shelf?"* the boy persisted, pointing and gazing at the object. *"Tell me."* The father was still earnestly occupied with completing his chore; and the child still trusted that the father would answer him, would share important knowledge with him. *"Tell me what's that!"* he repeated and ran over to inspect the object, with eagerness and curiosity. Now, from being indifferent, the father became annoyed.

"You ask me that question every time we come in here, Junior! It's a fire extinguisher. I've told you that a hundred times!"

It must be hard for a little boy to hear Father's angry voice and quick sharp words in response to a mere inquiry. But it is equally hard, and so frustrating not to know the fascinating things all around you—the shape and color, and strange names of real things within reach. *Fire extinguisher* —what, oh what could that be? The little boy will no doubt ask again, for little children are quite persistent in their eagerness to learn.

Photograph by Cobb Shinn

Our Nursery School class went on a brief walk recently. As usual, the children came back with treasures—this time in the form of sticks. Several children held on to little piles of sticks, and one child said, with sudden recollection of something he has heard, *"You can make a fire with sticks. Can you make a fire?"* He uttered the word "fire" with wide-eyed wonder. So we arranged to make a diminutive bonfire outdoors from the gathered sticks. The children began to pop questions on all sides. And what questions!

"Can fire hurt you?" — There was some fear and a sense of caution in that question.

"What will happen to the sticks from the fire?" This was genuine scientific inquiry.

47

"*How do you* make *a fire?*" This was manifestation of interest in skill. No abstract words would answer such questions. So, with the teacher's control and guidance the children arranged a circle of bricks and brought a can of water, answering the need for protection against fire. They seated themselves at a proper distance and handed the teacher the sticks, watching with great awe and wonder the piling of sticks and paper, the lighting of a match, the flame, the sparks—nothing escaped them, you may be sure.

"*I see smoke!*" exclaimed one. Another one blinked, and said with surprise, "*The smoke goes in my eyes.*"

"*Look, the fire is bigger!*"

"*I* smell *the fire!*" Another child put his hand out tentatively, "*It feels hot on my hand.*" Then the children took turns holding a hand close to the fire and feeling the warmth on a cold day.

Now the fire was dying out, and the children pointed to the small mounds of grey ashes and wanted them scooped up.

"*Make another fire,*" they begged (how natural it is to regret a dying fire!) but we had to put it out and poured water on it. Another new sensation to add to learning.

"*I hear it sizzle.*"

"*It smells different now.*"

How intense is the children's eagerness to learn, and how completely concrete is their way of learning, with all the senses alert. Things learned this way are not easily forgotten.

This Habit Business

By LOVISA WAGONER

It is a good thing for an adult from time to time to acquire some new skill so that he can watch himself as he learns. He sees himself fumble, make all sorts of unnecessary and awkward movements. Finally he, "gets the hang of it." Suddenly he is able to go through the whole series and has accomplished a new skill. He has the advantage over the young child in that he is able to keep the end in view. But even so he often includes unnecessary and inefficient movements. This is the way he learned and this is the way he performs. The comic routine, the elaborate leading up to a tiny and not very melodious note is a laughter-provoking device used by the professional entertainer or the amateur funnyman. If we could watch ourselves go through some of the routines of daily living we might find that in all seriousness we go through all manner of irrelevant antics. Neither money nor time can be spent more than once, and time really is all we have. We cannot afford to waste it.

Why do children dawdle in dressing in the morning? Why does a child wait after he has put on one sock before he puts on the other? Logically, the cue for putting on the second shoe, would be putting on the first shoe. Yet this seems to be true only occasionally. If we watch ourselves we will see that most of us put on one stocking and one shoe first. Just why, has not been perfectly explained, but it is obvious that this practice speeds up the dressing process.

This is the way we learn to follow a certain sequence in the routine of daily living. Such a sequence is not always economical, for an unnecessary step may be included which may actually hinder smooth performance. In this dawdling-during-the-dressing process, a child seems to find it easier to include pauses in the series of activities. When he is learning to dress himself, these pauses give him a chance to rest. As the child becomes more skillful, he uses up less energy and no longer needs rest periods. He is able to manage his clothes easily, but still includes the pauses. Now that he can dress himself easily, the pause gives him an opportunity for playing. His attention is attracted by something which has no connection with dressing; the dressing, no longer of any interest, is interrupted; the child plays with a toy or runs around the room. He is able to dress himself but is not yet quite skillful enough to do it efficiently.

One way of helping a child learn a sequence as a unit is to give him directions for the next step just as he is completing the preceding step. As he becomes a little more skillful he can keep in mind a second direction so that he is told "*Do this and this.*" Before long he is able to hold in mind three directions, "*Do this, then this, then this.*" Of course a parent should see that a child carries out the two or three steps without interruption. In the hurry of the morning it is easy to give directions but not easy to keep an eye on what the child is doing to make sure that the directions are followed.

It will pay any parent to watch himself go through an activity which he wants his child to learn so that he has in mind the steps which lead to completion of that task. It is a good idea also to take time not only to show him *how* to do something but to give him the help he needs and no more.

Parents often give directions to their child which he doesn't listen to. The child may seem disobedient since he does not respond or do what the parent has asked; the child may be so busy with what he is doing that the directions make no impression on him. Actually he does not hear. If directions are to be heeded they must be given in such a way that they are *understood* and must be given to a *listening child*. The first, most important and frequently disregarded rule about giving directions is to be sure the child is listening. Many children are very skillful in giving the *appearance of listening*; for that matter so are adults. Mother says "John" and John automatically says, "Yes, Mother?" Then his mind goes back to what was keeping it so busy and the direction goes "in one ear and out the other."

Because adults also are preoccupied they are apt to give directions off the top of the mind, paying little attention to reception conditions on the part of the child and even failing to notice for the moment whether that direction is obeyed. Later it dawns on the adult that he has been "disobeyed," or rather is "*un-obeyed*."

We expect children to respond to what is in our minds and we forget that they, like the household pet, follow the pattern of behavior they have found to be successful and, like the pet, obey cues which the adult may be unaware of giving as a signal. Although often managed almost as pets are managed, children are adults-to-be and are capable of complexity of learning which is the distinctive characteristic of human beings.

Edward Lettau

Good Taste Begins Early

By JAMES L. HYMES, JR.

Young children baffle many people. Do these little youngsters think? Do they feel? Do they know anything?

Face to face with a two-year-old or a three- or a four- or a five- some adults get a sinking feeling. What do I do now? What does he expect? And the sinking feeling leads to a kind of nervousness. Eager to please, but uncertain, some adults make funny faces or they talk "baby talk." They snap their fingers in front of children's noses; they talk louder (as though they were trying to make a foreigner understand); often they make a body-attack — swooping down to scoop the youngster up, poking him a little, tickling.

Unless you know young children —unless you live with them and watch them and see the world through their eyes—it is hard to believe that they are real. Hard to feel that anything is going on inside. Hard to know that anything matters. And if something does, what does?

Watch little children, however, and you know: life is real and life is earnest. Even very young ones are engaged in serious work . . . and it matters tremendously to them.

These young children are trying to make sense out of their world. They are trying to know all of its pieces and to fit the pieces together. They want to know the world's sounds and sights; the feel of its parts, their smell and their taste. Young children want to know what things do and what they can do with things.

What is going on inside? Something very real. These early years are years of great and wonderful discovery. The playing with fingers at the very beginning is a part of it; the sucking of toes; that irritating business of throwing toys out of the crib (Do they go away? Will they come back? Is there a noise?). The deep urge to put everything in your mouth is a part of it: buttons, match pads, dirt, the caps of milk bottles. . . . The hair-pulling of two-year-olds fits in here (Does hair come out? Will it break? Does pulling it hurt? What do people do?). The dipping of fingers-into-foods, the stepping into puddles. . . . Always: what is this world like? What are its textures and its temperatures, its sizes and shapes and sounds and odors? What is the real and what can it do?

Even the very smallest children are not "just cute" . . . and empty. These early years are not an idle waiting; they are the beginning of their knowing. Once you see this you know what these children basically want. You know one of the ingredients for their tip-top growth.

What is it that these young children need? Call it *quality* if you will. Quality in what they see. Quality in what they hear and touch and feel. They need purity in color. They need clarity in sound. They need cleanness in design. They need to be surrounded by the strong and the fine, the simple and the straightforward. This is what the beginning years of life can take and use and make a part of itself.

Are you going to buy a phonograph record for a young child? Don't think that the tone doesn't

51

splash of color. This young age is when you want good design, a fine feel to the wood or the cloth, colors that fit and are clear. This is when you want *quality*.

The same is true of books. The rightness of the colors, the accuracy and simplicity of the pictures, the goodness of the feel of the paper. the strength of the design, the internal trueness of the story: these are the things that count.

And this is what you take children to see. They want action, yes. And they like noise. But this doesn't have to equal the piling up of confusion.

Quality—good color, clear sound, fine form, good feel—the first seeing of the basic things in life—these need not cost more than the careless, the flashy, the gaudy, the cheap. Nor need they mean: "This is so fine you can only look at it from a distance," or "You have to be gentle with this because it will break."

Quality is not an expensiveness. It is not a delicateness or a trickiness that costs extra money. Quality for youngsters is the simple, the natural, the strong and the sturdy and the fine. It is the "X" that enables them to know at the start the basic things in their world, and then later, to be free to explore its shades and shadings off. Once you know that children need this, you can search it out and find it. It is all around for children to use.

matter "because he is so young." This is when the melody should be clear, the instruments distinct, the reproduction bell-like. This is when voices should be true. This is not the time for trashy confusion and scratches. These are the years for the foundation of taste.

Are you going to buy a musical toy—a play piano, a triangle, a drum or a xylophone? Make sure the instrument sounds good. Go seeking for a decent tone and a valid musical sound. This is not the time for tinny-tinkly jangles. If that ever has to be, let it come later.

Are you going to buy a doll or a wagon or a boat? Don't look for something gaudy with a cheap

---

My neighbor's child playfully called me Lee in front of my 4-year-old son. After she left, my youngster remarked about it.

"That's nothing," I told him. "Would you like to call me Lee sometimes?"

"Oh, no," he assured me seriously. "Then I wouldn't have anyone to call Mother."

—Mrs. Lee E. Berry
Magazine Digest.

Help Your Child to Help Himself

By MARY COOPER WALTON

By the time a child is two, walking and talking with ease, he has a strong urge to be self-reliant. This urge begins much earlier than we parents sometimes realize. Even babies try to help themselves, holding out a foot for a sock, or putting up an arm for a sleeve. But at around two the child suddenly wants to do more and more *for* himself and *by* himself. When he shows signs of wanting to help, it is important to give him freedom and encouragement. It is a golden opportunity for parents. Sympathetic support from mothers and fathers at this time gives the child the best kind of emotional satisfaction now, and assures a good foundation for a real and right independence in maturity.

Because the child has been so completely dependent on us up until now, it is easy to continue the habit of doing everything for him. But if we keep on with this habit the child may easily become either a raging bundle of frustration, or a heap of apathy. It is so much quicker and easier to get those clothes on ourselves! Yes, but there is no quick or easy cure for frustration or apathy. When a three-year-old shouts "Let me!" as he arrives, in dressing, at his overalls, it is hard for a mother to stand back and let him do it. Tugging and puffing, he usually gets both feet down one leg on the first try. After disentanglement and a fresh start, he will work hard at it again. And as he rises to be buttoned, his triumphant crow, "I did it all by myself," is a real reward for your moments of patience.

A mother should also look at the child's life through his eyes. Shelves, towel racks, hooks and washbasins at shoulder height must seem as high as mountains to him. It is a wonder he even wants to try to help himself! There is much we can do to set the stage. A low towel rack, closet hooks and bars moved within reach, a shoe bag on the door will lead him to the engrossing tasks of hanging up his

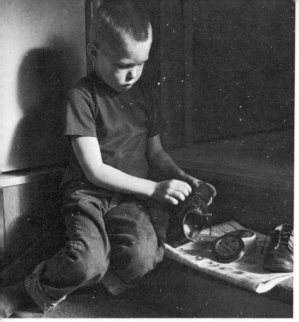

put away his toys at night. Pulling his own weight co-operatively in the family makes him feel important.

We can't expect, and should never demand, top performance in this "helpfulness." Fatigue, colds, or just plain "being little" will occasionally bring back the call of "Help me!" Then we should always help. Also, children vary in the ways they strive for independence. A three-year-old may be eager, and capable, in scraping carrots, setting the table, or putting away laundry, but may still need a lot of help in dressing. One day the same three-year-old will announce that she can dress herself alone—and she will! We must not be discouraged if enthusiasm for a task wanes. A child at this age is too young for consistency; but each thing accomplished is another step in learning more self-reliance.

In helping the child to help himself we must first follow his lead, letting him do what he can when he wants to help, and then make opportunities that suggest further ways of helping. Building self-reliance means a loosening of the apron strings. Mothers may feel a twinge, but the sturdy "bounce" of a happy, independent child who manages himself well is worth all of our efforts.

towel and putting away his pajamas and slippers. A low step stool, or a simple wooden grocery box, encourages greater independence in the bathroom. He will need a little supervision at first. But the day the child gets up from his nap, goes to the toilet, climbs up to the washbasin, washes his face and hands—and probably brushes his teeth for good measure—"all by himself," is one of the great thrills of his young lifetime.

When this "let me" stage begins, the child can now have a small pitcher for pouring his own milk. With a damp clean cloth readily available, he can wipe up his own spills. With a whisk broom and dustpan on a convenient hook, he can sweep up those peripatetic peas and crumbs from under his table. All of this is "real work" to the child and it is deeply satisfying.

More "real work" can come from little jobs and errands in the daily family routine. With a swagger of self-reliance, the two- and three-year-old can empty ash trays or waste baskets, put away all the slippers, set out the milk bottles, carry a package home from the store, and with help,

Self-Reliance—For What Purpose?

By DALE B. HARRIS

If one were to ask professional persons in child guidance what the most important aim of child rearing is, most would probably agree that it is the development of self-reliance. Psychiatrists remind us that one of their most common patients is the emotionally immature adult. Emotional immaturity is often expressed as a continued childish dependence on other adults for guidance and for decisions which the self-reliant adult should be making for himself.

We hear much today about cooperation, group dynamics, the importance of collective action. "Individualism" is decried as out of place in an interdependent world. Self-reliance as an emphasis in child training is not aimed at a kind of individualism which will tolerate the exploitation of people, nor is it aimed at individualism which assumes a "let-well-enough-alone" policy. A sound emphasis on self-reliance holds that each child should develop his potential as an individual in order that he may make his unique contribution to social action. It emphasizes equality of opportunity and sees the self-reliant individual as one who asks no special favors other than the provision of opportunity and facilities with which he can work to develop his own growth potential.

A modern developmental view of the child regards every normal infant as equipped with three strong motives: the potential for physical growth; an appetite for learning, so that the development of new skills becomes pleasurable; and a strong curiosity to manipulate experience, gain new ideas, and make new discoveries. No child must be forced into life; he runs out to meet it eagerly. He starts with zeal and interest. If discouragement and diffidence appear, it is because he acquires them.

Thus, self-reliance and independence can come easily and naturally to a child. Much of his behavior shows his strong desire to "do for himself." His insistence on dressing himself, his desire to help Mommy or Daddy when "help" may not be desired, his wish to "dress up" and play house, his wish to spend his nickel "all by himself" all bespeak this intense desire to grow up.

It is easy to foster such a desire, if an understanding parent recognizes its import and has a strong sense of confidence in the child's capacity to grow. It is easier to work with than against the child's course of development. The parent who sees only the weakness of the child in contrast with the complexity and forbiddingness of the world calls out warnings, insists on doing "for" the child. While it may be easy for the parent to follow his own doubts and anxiety, he usually must overcome his child's resistance to his help unless he has already beaten down the child's impulses to independent action.

Not that children's "will to grow" asserts itself on all occasions and with equal strength. Psychologists recognize that some child personalities give in more readily than others to persistent adult domination. There is the "strong-willed" child, and there is the "easy to manage" child. Every child, no matter how well respected as a person and how self-confident he is becoming, needs at times the reassurance of being helped at something he can perfectly well accomplish unaided. These temporary regressions to a less mature attitude come to all of us at times. The wise parent recognizes them as evidence of temporary emotional needs and gives the aid sought. He is actually giving emotional reassurance, not denying the child a learning experience or stultifying his emotional development. He does not become disturbed unless he sees the temporary regression becoming a permanent feature of the child's living. This is very unlikely to happen in a child who is generally encouraged to solve the problems he discovers or sets for himself.

This point of view does not assume that children never need guidance or restraint. The child acquires wisdom; it is not inherent in his disposition to grow. The parent's job is to work with, not against, the child's impulse to grow up, providing experience and opportunities to learn skills which help the child "do for himself," whether it be in physical performance or in moral choice. Guidance and sometimes restraint are necessary; nagging criticism and never-ceasing curbs are not serviceable in producing this end.

What are some of the things parents do, often out of affection, which hinder the development of self-reliance? They over-emphasize the danger in new learning situations instead of the thrill of mastery. They forbid the child's handling tools for fear he may hurt himself instead of giving a few instructions on how tools may be handled safely. They try to "save time" by dressing the child instead of allowing him time and encouragement to handle his own clothing. They supervise closely his play and choice of companions instead of attempting to foster the skills and interests which will insure the child's activities in constructive ways with desirable companions. They interfere in childish quarrels, attempt to straighten out the slightest problems with the neighbors or at school instead of watching the child work his own way through his difficulties, with appropriate encouragement and guidance. *"You can't do it; let Mommy help"* becomes an oft-repeated phrase, instead of *"You're doing nicely; I'm sure you can finish it."*

We say that encouragement and praise are great aids in the development of the child's skill, initiative, and self-reliance. How many of us as parents truly learn the nice art of appreciating the values which come to the child from his performance? Can we honestly recognize in the young child's crude woodwork the splendid boat he sees there, and enjoy it with him, without either dashing his sense of achievement by rebuilding it for him, or conveying to him a patronizing tolerance of his efforts by insincere praise? It is so important for adults to learn to understand the values children find in their experience. Out of such appreciation, which is the fine art of parenthood, the child's self-reliance grows quite naturally.

The young daughter paid her mother the highest compliment when she introduced her as a speaker at a Mother and Daughter banquet, by saying, "She's my mother. I had nothing to say about that. But I can choose my friends, and she's first on the list."

—Friendly Chat

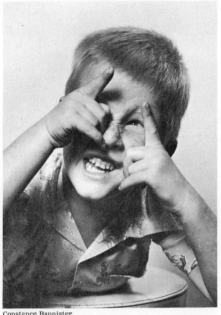

Constance Bannister

Imaginative Play
in the
Preschool Years

By MARGARET ROHNER LINDMAN

"I don't want my child wasting his time playing," said Mrs. Birney. "There are so many practical things in the world he needs to learn."

"Where is your child?" she was asked.

Mrs. Birney replied, "Right there in the buggy."

The tiny baby in the buggy turned its wide green eyes on the adults and seemed to plead for someone to "come play with me."

Mrs. Jones didn't realize that one of the most practical things she can do for her child is to engage in imaginative play with him. Play is an essential part of life. All human beings need play. To deny play to a child is to deprive him of many of his finest opportunities for learning. Children learn through play.

Imaginative play stimulates the child's mind. He becomes more alert, remembers more clearly, and is encouraged to develop his creative potential. Imaginative play provides a wholesome release from the tension of everyday life.

What a delightful feeling of closeness and joy arises between mother and baby as mother plays "This little piggy went to market — This little piggy stayed home —" while washing baby's toes. The shared play in "Pat-a-cake pat-a-cake baker's man —" charms most young children. These and other simple finger plays are one of the ways a parent can introduce a child to the delightful world of make-believe.

Nursery rhymes, jingles, and songs such as "Jack Be Nimble," "Humpty Dumpty," and "Little Miss Muffet" are filled with playfulness, nonsense, and the ridiculous (who ever heard of an entire army trying to piece together a broken egg — Humpty Dumpty). Yet this very material introduces the child to rhythm, interesting sounds of language, and an enriched vocabulary.

Frequently the best rhymes, jingles, and refrains are those which are improvised by a parent to fit some household situation or some event in the

57

child's life. This is a pleasant way for adults and children alike to recall information. This fact is recognized by commercial advertisers and explains why advertisements are so often jingles.

The young child is a great imitator. He imitates noises he hears, sounds, words, and inflections of speech. As he grows, he imitates the movement he observes. As his experiences increase, he pretends to be the people he knows and to re-enact the experiences that have impressed him. He may pretend to be father, mother, the family pet, the milkman, or the mailman. Through this play he tries on the life about him.

Observant parents can do much to stimulate and guide this dramatic play. Father can ask the pint-sized mailman to deliver a letter to mother. Mother can provide her young would-be homemaker with safe utensils for mixing imaginary pies and cakes — and even have an imaginary taste of these delicacies. Instead of ignoring, correcting, or interrupting these flights into the imaginary, the wise parent enters into the play and thereby subtly guides and expands the child's thoughts.

It is true that inspiration flows best from a prepared mind. The child needs to acquire information. Parents expand his world by offering him a wide variety of experiences that are suitable to his interests, background, and stage of development. Walks around the block and trips to the nearby park and to the store are suitable early childhood experiences. As the child develops, visits to a farm or zoo, the library, museums, and other places are meaningful. These real experiences are supplemented and extended through discussion about them with the child and through literary experiences.

Stories and poems read and told to the child build his cultural background and provide an important basis for imaginative play.

As the child matures socially, individual dramatic play will be replaced by group dramatic play. The parent can encourage such play by helping the children think of wholesome dramatic possibilities for enactment by suggesting characterizations and by furnishing interesting imaginative play materials. These materials need not be expensive. Dress-up clothes such as mother's discarded costume jewelry, her aprons, father's colorful but old ties, vests, and other belongings are perfect accessories for clowns, pirates, chefs, and queens. Blocks, both large and small, as well as giant and tiny boxes are just the items required by the young child. Because these items are so flexible and usable in many situations, they are sometimes referred to as *ambiguous stimuli*. The reactions one may have to ambiguous stimuli are unpredictable and may cause one to find meaningful relationships between previously unrelated experiences and feelings.

Imaginative games and experiences should continue to be shared with children as they grow older. Children need to be encouraged to explore all the possibilities before they make a creative decision. They need to feel free to express unusual ideas, even if only half developed or if silly-sounding at first. Parents can encourage flexibility in children by rewarding many responses rather than a right response, by encouraging many questions rather than expecting perfect answers, by looking for humor (not ridicule) in life situations, and by being ready for the unexpected. This attitude encourages and develops the imagination of the young and can make the life of the parent more fun.

You Build Imagination

By JAMES L. HYMES, JR.

Imagination in our children! Here is a quality we all seek. The power to dream new ideas, to picture new relationships and arrangements, to create—words, objects, sounds, colors — the new and unique that has never existed before.

We want it for our children for its own sake. Imagination gives a magic touch to life, a lift and a lilt.

above her neighbors, one grocery store more attractive and appealing, one magazine more exciting to read. With our children's future in mind we all train for certain skills that will pay later. Here is one—the freedom and the power to think brave new thoughts — that we must not overlook.

For imagination is built into chil-

It picks up the humdrum and the routine, the ordinary, and raises even the everyday into something of the extraordinary. Children with imagination get more fun out of their living and they bring more fun *to* their living, more plain simple enjoyment. This is worth prizing, for itself and for children.

But imagination has a tangible, practical importance in the work-a-day world, too. Here is an asset that business seeks, that pays dividends in politics, that the arts and the professions want. This is the touch that makes one homemaker stand out

dren. It doesn't just happen. Some lucky ones are not blessed and others passed over. Children can be imaginative and they can carry their creative ways with them into life, if we help them.

How? One mistaken idea has taken strong root. It is the notion that you make children creative by feeding them the fanciful. Bring them up on a diet of the unreal—the myth, the figurative, the wild-eyed—and supposedly you stir their own creative dreaming. Children have been read and told stories about giants and fairies and trolls and witches, about princes and pixies, gnomes and leprechauns — all with this notion in mind.

But children themselves do not bear out this approach. From the very beginning they imagine—not at all out of the unreal and the untrue —but only out of the sternest, strictest, toughest stuff of reality. Look at two- and three- and four-year-olds and see what they make believe: the things they know best and most thoroughly, from the closest first-hand observation. They pretend they are mothers and daddies and babies; they pretend they are sleeping and eating and washing and ironing and drinking (they even make believe they are spanking!); it is the "playing house" that is the start of it all. The life that has been over and over again flowing into them first comes out in their dramatic play. Children themselves are saying: you can only be imaginative on the firmest base of reality. The thing you know best is what you are creative with.

Of course, more than children tell us, this is true. Our new surgical techniques are not stumbled on by amateurs but are creatively developed by informed doctors who really know their anatomy. New harmonies and rhythms are not hit on luckily by beginners but they grow out of the deep familiarity of the highly trained musician. Our most forward-reaching scientific theories and bravest interpretations of our physical world come only from those who are really steeped in their disciplines.

Yet we have a hard time believing this for children. With them we follow a thin dish-watery approach: no facts, no depth, no richness, no real knowing. It is the light, the fluffy, the frothy, the bubbly: animals who speak, events that couldn't happen, powers that don't exist! These do not give youngsters the stuff they need for their fullest creative thinking and playing.

Imagination has many ingredients but here at least is one: *facts*, truth, reality. Children must *know* if they are to be able to go on into the unknown. If we want to develop good creative adventuresome thinking and doing. one part of our job is clear: let us give youngsters, from the very beginning, real living, real experiencing. real seeing and tasting and smelling and hearing. Let us take youngsters to see trains and ferries and boats and trucks; machines and buses and tractors and planes, filling stations and sawmills and firehouses. bakery stores and markets. . . Let us give them the chance to be with and talk with and watch the real people who do the real jobs that make our real world go. If we can feed this rich flow into them, at least they have one ingredient for an imaginative output of their own.

Let us get into their reading — when they are young in the stories we read and tell to them; when they are older in the stories they read for themselves—books that carry ideas, books that have content, books that can extend and push deeper what they have been able to see for themselves. Let us surround them with pictures—simple yet clear and detailed—that make the life around them more vivid and more meaningful. Let us, in the talking we do even with young children, make our own words add to their understanding of the true world.

For there has to be a richness of "coming-in" before there can be a richness of "giving-out." And these are fuels we use: trips, people, books, pictures, words. . . Enough of these and youngsters at least have a basis for creating for themselves.

Teach Your Child To Share

By KATHERINE REEVES

Can you remember what it felt like to be bursting with a secret? Or what it felt like to want to give someone part of your treasure so much that it almost hurt? When you felt that way you had discovered the wonderful joy of sharing.

Sharing is more than a social grace. It is a deep, spiritual experience. It unites or divides families, neighborhoods and nations. The desire to share, and the understanding of what it means to share can be taught, in the sense that they can be imparted to children through the habits of family living. There are many *do's,* and a few *don'ts* for you to think about, if you want to help your children learn to share.

Begin early to put meaning into the word "share" and the idea "sharing": The parent who is truly generous in spirit with a child communicates the real meaning of sharing far better than a thousand explanations do.

When Tim brings you a sticky piece of candy from the birthday party, or when Mary tells you of something important that happened in school, or picks a bunch of dandelions for the dinner table, do you show your appreciation for the love and feeling that inspired the deed— "Thank you for sharing this."?

How often a child's spontaneous gift to a grownup is met with some such careless comment as "Go wash that sticky mess off your hands," or "Take that bunch of weeds back outdoors." Haven't you seen that happen? And Tim goes obediently to wash his hands, and gives his little

H. Armstrong Roberts

brother a shove on the way, just because he has to get rid of his disappointment somehow.

Use the word to explain the deed: When you have seen your child give his cherished toy to another child, without being prompted; or divide his cookie with his brother, without being asked, do you share *your* pride in his spontaneous giving? Do you give him a word that fits his action— "It was friendly of you to share. . ."?

Help him know that sharing is a spiritual act: Sharing need not stay on the level of material possessions or benefits. You can share another person's trouble, and his joy. You can share an idea. Sharing is as much a matter of feeling as it is doing.

Let the act of sharing be its own reward: The temptation may be great, when you see your child acting in a truly generous way with another to overdo your approval of his behavior. Elizabeth Harrison, an early worker in childhood education in the United States, gave this rule to mothers and young women who would be teachers—"Never reward a spiritual deed with a material gift." This is a good rule to remember. Give a smile, or a word, instead of a lollipop.

Help him keep a wholesome balance: Sharing is an act of independence. But looking after one's own needs realistically is also part of development toward independence. The too-generous person may really turn out to be selfish, for he may be depriving another person of the privilege of solving some of his own important problems himself. There is a real balance to be preserved between giving and withholding. Sometimes it is more difficult, but more necessary, to give of one's self rather than of one's possessions.

Do not force sharing: Sharing is one of the amenities of the social world. Grownups are often so eager to have children understand that sharing is important, socially, that admonition starts far too early — "Share your dolly"; "Share your cookie." But the words have little meaning until life puts content into them.

The idea of what it means to share, in desire and deed, is a slow-growing idea. Do not force a very young child to part with his treasure before he knows what it means to share. Such forcing gets across the idea that, "They're taking this away from me" rather than the idea that, "I'm giving part of this because I want to."

Help him know himself: When a child persistently refuses to share anything—his mother, or his truck, or his ice cream, or his love—do not increase his burden of insecurity with blame. Look below his surface actions to the source of his fear. Undue hoarding of anything means that anxiety is present. Help him know that he will not lose, but gain, by giving. Work slowly to reassure him, to help him build values that include other people and their needs along with his own.

Edward Lettau

THE MIRACLE OF LIVING THINGS fascinates the child as she learns about her world.

Nature and Human Nature

A Must for Your Children

By EDITH E. MADDOX

In order to have success and enjoyment with nature experiences, the following hints may prove helpful. When handling pets for the first time, provide the youngsters with gloves or mittens to avoid being scratched or bitten while becoming accustomed to the pet's maneuvers. Also, a small basket or box in which to hold the new creature saves the animal from being unduly squeezed, yet permits stroking and fondling. Ample "bedding," be it excelsior, sawdust, hay or newspaper, makes all cleaning easier.

Do not expect young children to be interested in collections for very long. While most youngsters are veritable scavengers, love to collect, and want help in arranging and displaying their finds, their interest wanes because there is no element of change. Nothing happens. So a new collection is started and, as a rule, the old one can be subtly discarded without ever being missed.

Did you know that the *activities* of gardening are more fun than the results? Digging, raking, sprinkling, these are the real joys. Finding grubs or an old boot are adventures. But stepping on a seedling or pulling up a choice specimen often dampens all gardening pleasures. So provide digging areas in preference to garden space if both are not available. Or plant a narrow border between sidewalk and house so that there is an obvious space for stepping. It is interesting to force a variety of flowering branches indoors, or watch the roots develop on beans placed between a damp blotter and a glass jar. For apartment dwellers, a row of cigar box gardens is close and personal.

Sometimes children lose zest for a wonderful nature experience because of some minor unpleasant factor. If you know the child is likely to be annoyed, it is well to help him anticipate and minimize these less agreeable aspects. For example, if you are going for a tramp through the meadows in the autumn, mention that there might be burrs, but to watch out for them; and remark that if he gets into them you will lend a hand. Or when riding a horse for the first time, say that most animals have odors about

them but that you soon get accustomed to them. If chicks are about to hatch, point out that the interior of an egg is damp and sticky, so the newly-hatched chick will not appear sprightly and fluffy, but "something like you look when you're having a shampoo," until it has a chance to dry.

Considerable understanding is achieved by opening growing bulbs, eggs, seed pods, cocoons, so that children may see what goes on during the waiting periods. This is often a revelation to adults, too.

If each parent is alert to his own child's questions, there will be opportunities to clear up many hazy notions through simple experiments, and have a very rewarding time of it. It is revealing to try out freezing and thawing, to see what sinks and floats, what responds to a magnet, or measure how much rain fell during the night.

Every home does not have to be a zoo, nor every child become a Burbank or an Edison, but he does need a wealth of science experiences in order to understand this world in which he lives.

Edward Lettau

What Would You Do About
LITTLE HURT, BIG FUSS?

By RALPH K. MEISTER

Little Jeanette, age two, always cries and makes a big fuss over even the slightest bump or hurt, to the point that it is sometimes embarrassing.

If you were Jeanette's parents, what would you do?

a. Scold her mildly for being careless.

b. Shame her by calling her a "cry-baby."

c. Comfort and soothe her briefly but do not dote on her complaint. Then send her off to play, "like a big girl."

d. Ignore her crying and send her to another room if it persists.

e. Praise her when she does not cry.

f. Cuddle her but insist that she does not return to the activity in which she got hurt.

H. Armstrong Roberts

Discussion

Children at this age, just outgrowing babyhood, will use any likely excuse to get attention either in the form of parental concern or babying by the parent. The child still needs a certain amount of cuddling to help her in this transitional period. However, running to Mother at the slightest hurt is not the most socially desirable means of securing it. A combination of responses (c) and (e) would probably be the best method of handling this situation since neither magnifies her hurt nor denies a certain minimum of consolation while encouraging a more mature attitude. Responses (a), (b), and (d) tend to squelch her too abruptly and might have repercussions in other kinds of attention-getting behavior. (f), on the other hand, suggests a parental over-concern that may further encourage the crying. In general, our goal is to help the child to take the ordinary bumps and bruises in her stride and a combination of (c) and (e) seems most likely to promote such an attitude.

What Would You Do About
THE PEOPLE DOWNSTAIRS?

By RALPH K. MEISTER

Tommy, age two, has been running heavy-footedly from one room to another and mother has asked him a number of times to stop running to keep from disturbing the people downstairs.

If you were Tommy's mother, what would YOU do?

(a) Give Tommy another warning and spank him if he does not stop running.

(b) Stop Tommy forcibly and make him sit in a chair for about five minutes to calm down.

(c) Remove his shoes so he is less noisy and allow him to run.

(d) Take time out and engage him in play until he has forgotten about this particular activity.

(e) Take Tommy out for an hour or more each day so that he can get

H. Armstrong Roberts

his fill of large muscle exercise and is tired enough so he will not be charging around the house.

(f) Let him run but appeal to the good nature of the people downstairs, should the issue of his noisiness arise.

Discussion

Modern apartments and even two-flat dwellings were assuredly not designed with the needs of their youngest occupants in mind. Most city dwellers face this problem in one form or another. Children are not always quiet in their growing-up activities so any solution is at best a compromise.

Neither alternative (a) or (b) is desirable even though it may be suspected that they are most often used. A child of Tommy's age needs this kind of exercise for his own development of such motor skills. (d) is not particularly practical; not only is it unfeasible to drop everything and engage the child in play but, even further, there is no assurance that Tommy will not want to run after he is through with the sedentary play. By all means use method (e) if you are an apartment dweller or live where the inside activity of the child must be somewhat restricted. For the slightly older child, a nursery school group with playground activity is highly desirable. Ordinarily, (e) will not tire the child nor is it desirable to exhaust him. Therefore (c) is the approved home-front alternative. As for (f), if the people downstairs bring up the issue in the first place, there may not be too much good nature to which you can appeal.

What Would You Do About
THE SHARP KNIFE?

By RALPH K. MEISTER

Arthur, age two, has just taken a very sharp knife from the table and is going off to play with it.

If you were Arthur's mother, what would YOU do?

(a) Run after Arthur and get the knife away from him as soon as possible.

(b) Follow him and take the knife away when he becomes distracted or bored with it.

(c) Offer to trade him the knife for something else less lethal.

(d) Ask him to return the knife to you upon threat of spanking.

(e) Ignore him until you can get the knife away by a surprise move that will avoid the danger of a struggle.

Discussion

Certain situations are potentially dangerous for two-year-olds. Since they do not always realize the danger, rather prompt and unquestioning obedience on their part has much to recommend it. Therefore, in this particular crisis as in other comparable ones, alternative (d) seems the method of choice. The child has to learn the times you "mean business" and a few severe spankings may be necessary to instill this valuable item of information in his repertoire of interpretations. (a) and (e) run the risk of increasing the likelihood that someone will be hurt; (b) prolongs the agony; (c) may be used for a particular time to get out of one specific spot but is not a method to be used repeatedly or generally. These situations call for a wholeheartedly autocratic parent who brooks not even the possibility of refusal. Children last longer that way.

What Would You Do About A STICKY LOLLIPOP?

By RALPH K. MEISTER

George, age two, is out with his mother while she is visiting a friend. The friend's young daughter returns from school and George makes an appearance shortly thereafter, sporting a lollipop, a gift from the little girl. Mother is not concerned about what the lollipop will do to George's clothes but she can see sticky patches on her friend's furniture, her own clothes, etc.

If you were George's mother, what would YOU do?

(a) Tell the little girl that George can have candy only from you and give the lollipop back to her.

(b) Offer to store the lollipop for George until he gets home.

(c) Let George keep the lollipop but insist that he sit in a chair while eating it, taking it away from him should he try to wander off.

(d) Hold George on your lap and keep a tight rein on what he does with the lollipop.

(e) Suggest to the little girl that because of the drooling problem she give him a small bit of candy that he can pop into his mouth and which he does not have to hold in his hand.

(f) Terminate your visit.

Discussion

This is one of those delicate inter-personal situations which offers rich possibilities for doing the wrong thing no matter what we do. Let's consider the different possibilities. The only possibility to be strictly ruled out is (a), unless you do not mind being considered an ogre by the little girl and her mother. (b) is probably going to make George holler and fuss a lot and with some justification on his part. (d) is a rather gruesome prospect for the mother. Either (c) or (e) are here recommended to do justice to all concerned, to the hostess and her furniture, to her generous offspring and to your potentially messy boy. Of course, if all this seems too much, there is always (f) as an extreme but by no means impossible measure.

What Would You Do
WHEN THE CHILD UPSETS YOUR SCHEDULE?

By RALPH K. MEISTER

H. Armstrong Roberts

Richard, two-and-a-half years of age, refuses to let his mother dress him in the morning. He will insist on having his own way by trying, for instance, to put on one of his shoes by himself. This delays breakfast and is generally upsetting to the morning schedule.

If you were Richard's parents, what would *you* do?

a. Ignore his protests and proceed with the dressing, by force if necessary.

b. Make a game by playfully biting him on his toes if he does not let you put on the shoe.

c. Walk away from him to show your strong disapproval of his lack of cooperation.

d. Let him try to put the shoe on by himself and gently point out, "See, Richard can't do that."

e. Loosen the laces to make it easy for him to put on the shoe. Then help him with the final stages.

Discussion

Richard is showing that he has reached a new stage of his development. He is not being contrary but wants to practice a new and challenging task. Therefore, (e) would be the best way to handle the situation and Richard should actually be praised for whatever success he achieves. (a) would frustrate him while (d) would discourage him in his first attempts to develop a very necessary skill. (b) might get him dressed in a shorter time but would still be depriving him of an opportunity to learn. (c) is inappropriate since the situation calls for sympathetic understanding and approval rather than disapproval.

What Would You Do About
THE BOY WHO WANTS A DOLL?

By RALPH K. MEISTER

Ronnie, almost three, has requested a doll for his birthday. Father is reluctant to comply with this desire, feeling it will tend to make the boy a "sissy."

If you were Ronnie's father, what would YOU do?

H. Armstrong Roberts

a. Tell him that little boys are not allowed to play with dolls, that people would laugh at him.

b. Get him a doll but make it a cowboy doll or a doll dressed in male attire.

c. Try to drum up his interest in some other kind of toy before the day of reckoning arrives, maybe a kiddy-car he has always wanted.

d. Get him the doll as requested.

Discussion

Three is too early an age at which to choose the child's toys upon the basis of sex. Seven is an early enough age. Furthermore, a doll for the young child has much to recommend it as an appropriate toy. The child can use it to dramatize some parts of his own life. With a new baby in the family, for instance, the doll can take a lot of the spanking and normal aggression. The child can assume the dominant position of scolding the doll for wetting. All in all, it is a valuable prop for the child's dramatic play and would hardly constitute an influence toward making him a "sissy" unless all his other toys were systematically what we adults consider "girl stuff." Therefore, (d) would be the recommended procedure. (b) is an undesirable compromise because such a doll would have very little meaning for the child at this age. (a) constitutes an unfair denial of a legitimate area of interest and play. (c) might work to convince him he really does not want the doll but for all the reasons enumerated above, why try to sell him on this?

What Would You Do
ABOUT REPETITIVE SPEECH?

By MARGARET ROHNER LINDMAN

Kenny ran into the house. "M-m-m-m-mother," he shouted, "the ice-cream man-man-man is coming. Can I get-get-get-get some?"

Kenny's mother was concerned. She had noticed that he frequently repeated sounds and words.

"Is he a stutterer?" she puzzled.

If you were Kenny's mother, what would you do?

(a) Tell Kenny to stop "stuttering" and speak clearly.

(b) Try to anticipate the words he wanted to say and prompt him.

(c) Tell him to stop, think, and say the sentence over again—slowly.

(d) Act unconcerned, listen, and say nothing until Kenny is finished speaking.

(e) Repeat correctly all that Kenny said and have him imitate your speech.

(f) Pretend you can not hear what he said until he repeats his words fluently.

Discussion

Very few people are so fluent that they never have to hesitate or repeat speech sounds. During the course of our normal speech all of us repeat sounds and words with surprising frequency. We do not expect others to become concerned when we stumble in our speech, and Kenny doesn't expect his mother to criticize him either. Therefore (d) she should act unconcerned, listen, and say nothing until Kenny finishes speaking. To tell Kenny to stop "stuttering" (a) would label him as a stutterer and might create a lifelong emotional and speech problem for him. Today many speech therapists subscribe to the theory that children become stutterers AFTER someone has pinned that label on them. Stuttering is one of the most injurious terms a parent can apply to a child's speech. Responses (c), (e), and (f) are also unsatisfactory. Understandably, Kenny is in a hurry for an answer. To force him to take the time to reconsider his words or to imitate others would indicate a very unrealistic and unsympathetic approach to life on the part of the adult. These approaches could cause Kenny to become resentful or confused. Why is (b) unsatisfactory? Nothing is more annoying than to be constantly interrupted. It is belittling to have someone take your ideas and express them more quickly and better than you do. Haven't you, as an adult, been in this situation? Remember how you felt? The child's tensions and anxieties are often reflected in his speech. When Kenny's mother shows interest in his ideas she helps to relieve his inner tensions and, hopefully, he will find no need to continue his excessively repetitive speech. If Kenny's repetitive speech persists, his parents should discuss the problem with a qualified speech therapist.

What Would You Do About
THE CHILD WHO WILL NOT SHARE?

By RALPH K. MEISTER

Albert, age three, refuses to part with his toy rabbit that a neighborhood playmate, who was invited to play with him, has requested. The playmate, also age three, is a little "put out" but does not contest the possession probably because she does not feel she is on home territory.

If you were Albert's parents, what would YOU do?

a. Tell Albert he is very selfish and a naughty boy for not relinquishing his toy to his guest.

b. Take the toy from Albert by force and give it to his playmate.

c. Give his playmate another comparable toy and encourage them to continue playing.

d. Go into Albert's toy closet and offer his playmate the choice of any of the toys in it.

e. Engage both children in some kind of game so that Albert will lose interest in his rabbit and drop it.

f. Tell Albert his playmate will not give him any toys when he goes visiting.

Discussion

A situation of the sort described undoubtedly occurs so many times that answer (e), distracting both children by starting a game with them, would soon become more of a nuisance than the original problem. It is open to the additional objection that it introduces adult interference in a situation which children should learn to settle for themselves. (b) is not only too severe but unfair to Albert. Even invited playmates should wait their turn. (a) likewise is a form of pressure that may be premature. If his playmate refuses to play with Albert because Albert's attitude with regard to his toys has become overly possessive, this natural pressure will influence Albert eventually in the direction of greater generosity. (f) might be used with Albert later. At three such a threat may have little weight by comparison with the immediate possession of the rabbit. (d) may be less advisable than (c) since giving his playmate free access to Albert's toy closet may increase Albert's sense of possessiveness and make him less willing to share his toys. (c) would probably be the best measure.

What Would You Do About
BROKEN GLASSES?

By RALPH K. MEISTER

H. Armstrong Roberts

Patsy, age three, looks very cute wearing father's glasses except that this time she has dropped them and broken a lens.

If you were Patsy's parents, what would YOU do?

a. Scold her for being careless.

b. Forbid her ever to play with father's things.

c. Reassure her that the damage is not important so she does not get guilt feelings.

d. Make her help in cleaning up the debris by getting the dustpan or other clean-up equipment.

e. Tell her it is too bad but assume the blame for the accident yourself.

Discussion

We hate to say "we told you so" but that is pretty much the situation. Glasses, father's watch, his pipe, or anything breakable should not be entrusted to Patsy, however cute a figure she cuts with such an object. The basic irresponsibility rests with the adults. Therefore, (a) would be inappropriate as would (b) if it were stated in a manner as to suggest the child was to blame. (d) is poor, if it is presented as necessary expiation of Patsy's wrongdoing. (c) is hardly realistic. Actually the damage is rather serious and constitutes a nuisance. That leaves (e) as probably the fairest method of handling the situation. And this should constitute a lesson to parents. No?

What Would You Do About
A ROUGHHOUSE ACCIDENT?

By RALPH K. MEISTER

After a few minutes of rough-and-tumble play with Jerry, age three, father has returned to his cup of coffee and amused conversation with mother when Jerry charges around the corner to butt father and spills the cup of coffee, mostly over father.

If you were Jerry's father, what would YOU do?

a. Punish Jerry with a smart spank, on the spot.

b. Point out to him the damage he has done and lecture him against such rough tactics.

c. Mop up and charge off the incident to unavoidable accidents.

d. Avoid such rough-house play in the future.

e. Forbid Jerry to run in the house.

Ewing Galloway

f. Try to restrict such play to a special place, and after such exciting play give Jerry time to settle down with some calmer play.

Discussion

Consistency in parents is one of the necessary virtues. This was hardly an unavoidable accident (Alternative c.). It resulted from the fact that Jerry was not exactly aware that the rough-and-tumble play was over, and he was still carrying on. Therefore, spanking (a) or lecturing against rough tactics (b) are not quite fair. (e) is not to the point, nor is such an extreme measure as (d) necessary. A certain amount of rough-and-tumble is probably good play. However, we do owe it to Jerry and to ourselves to make it pretty plain to him when that part of the play is over. Therefore, (f) seems to be the preferable mode of handling this situation and of preventing its recurrence.

What Would You Do About
DESTRUCTIVE BEHAVIOR?

By RALPH K. MEISTER

JOHNNY, age three, is playing rather roughly with a large teddy bear he received as a present some time ago, pummeling it, kicking it and in between times threatening it with all kinds of violence. Mother is rather concerned about both the teddy bear, which was a fairly expensive present, and about Johnny's display of aggression. However, she is doubtful about how to handle this situation.

What Would You Do?

(a) Try to suggest more constructive play with the teddy bear, such as putting it to bed or dressing it up or something else less violent.

(b) Threaten to take the teddy bear away from Johnny if he continues to abuse it so.

(c) Point out to Johnny that if this is the kind of care he takes of a gift given to him, he is likely not to get any more.

(d) Let him continue but insist that he play in another room.

(e) Let him continue, "period."

Discussion

Assuming that the teddy bear is not actually being destroyed by this rough treatment but can withstand it, the problem posed in this quiz is actually more a problem of Mother's attitude than it is a problem of Johnny's behavior. In other words, we parents too often and too strongly frown on the display of normal, healthy aggression in the child. Such aggression may be the young child's demonstration to himself that he is not hopelessly helpless and can lash out in his own behalf, or it may be the child's attempt symbolically to express his anger at some real or fancied hurt. In the latter case questioning him in a noncritical and nonpreaching fashion may give us some insight into how he thinks and feels.

For all the above reasons, alternatives (a), (b), and (c) are not recommended because they attempt to suppress this normal aggression which has a very good symbolic outlet in the play with the teddy bear. (e) is the preferred alternative, i.e., just letting him continue. However, if Mother is rendered uncomfortable by this activity, alternative (d) may be used provided the request to play in another room is not suggested in a punishing or disapproving way.

Johnny is less likely to take some of this aggression out on his playmates or parents if he settles it in part with teddy bear.

Children, Music and You

By MARY L. BARRETT

TODAY, the world is filled with music. Music can travel with us in cars, planes, trains, and even on walks. Music is played in busy stores, train stations and industrial plants.

Research has discovered that music can be used beneficially as therapy in rehabilitation programs, for mental ills, in hospitals and doctors' offices. Music therapy is not new. It has been experimented with effectively for thousands of years.

Today, we cannot help but be "music-minded." We are not only surrounded by music but have access to a great variety of music. Children are subject to these extravagant variations which in a sense we control.

For children, music is all around them: in the thundering clouds of a rainy day, the fluttering of a moth on a lighted screen, the footsteps of Mother after an afternoon nap, the pounding of hands on an Indian drum, the jingling of bells around the neck, the rolling and the dancing, the crawling and the running, the expressive joy of feeling alive and secure in a comfortable world.

We want to have our children "feel at home" with music, to experience the aesthetic satisfaction of music which comes with feeling music in their arms and legs, in their singing and laughing, in their listening and appreciation.

Out of many sources, the record player is one which may bring to children a listening enjoyment of folk songs, symphonies, instrumental solos, quartets and all the recorded world of music to be heard, remembered and loved.

American Music Conference

It is essential that the record player be a good, substantial and satisfying one. You may find at the very beginning that your child will be more interested in the mechanics of operation than in the music itself. He may attend more tenaciously to the turning off and on of the player, the operation of the player arm and the needle, the whirling of the turntable than to the record which is playing. It is the learning process incipient to appreciative listening which comes soon. If the player is placed on the floor or a low table, the child can more easily learn the mechanics of this wondrous instrument. You will need and want to plan simple rules for the operation of the player so that listening time may be a relaxing, satisfying time for your child and you.

The selection of records for the most part is your responsibility. Be as sensitive and critical in the selection as you are with your own devoted collection. Many reliable sources are available to guide you in your selection.*

When your child has had the experience of creating his own songs and learning simple songs of the "here and now" around him and has then been introduced to the vast store of American folk songs, you will want to venture together into the folk music of the people of other cultures.

After an experience of seeing and touching instruments and hearing simple melodies played on them, one day your child will be "listening-

---

*Among the most complete is:
New York Library Association, Children's Young Adult Services Section. *Recordings for Children*. The Association. First published in 1961 and revised periodically.

ready" for the beauty of such instrumental recordings as "Saint-Saëns' *The Carnival of the Animals*, Bach's *Brandenburg Concerto No. 2* and Bartok's *Romanian Folk Dances*.

There are recordings for special holidays which express the rejoicings and gratitude of many people in celebrating unique occasions not to be forgotten.

There are times in the child's day when you may find recordings important, especially during days of illness and convalescence, during rest time before meals or similar occasions when the child chooses books and pictures for moments of relaxation.

Recorded music can become the threshold into a "world-home" of confident understanding, constant sensitivity and simple appreciation for our young children all over the land in which they may learn to communicate with each other through the language of music.

The Common Tasks

The common tasks are beautiful if we
Have eyes to see their shining ministry.
The plowman with his share deep in the loam;
The carpenter whose skilled hands build a home
The gardener working with reluctant sod,
Faithful to his partnership with God—
These are the artisans of life. And, oh,
A woman with her eyes and cheeks aglow,
Watching a kettle, tending a scarlet flame,
Guarding a little child—there is no name
For this great ministry. But eyes are dull
That do not see that it is beautiful;
That do not see within the common tasks
The simple answer to the thing God asks
Of any child, a pride within His breast;
That at our given work we do our best.
—GRACE NOLL CROWELL

(From *Songs of Hope*, copyright Harper and Brothers, publishers.)

Eva Luoma

BIG BROTHER TAKES PRIDE in introducing little brother to the beach. Jealous flareups between children in the family are normal, too.

Ewing Galloway

Morale in Childhood

By KATHERINE REEVES

Morale has been casually described as "a lot of little things." Whether we can precisely define the quality or not we all know what it means. It is a term most often applied to armies, perhaps, or to groups of people faced with grave problems of feeling and action. But it has an individual meaning too. And its synonym is *spirit*. It is in the sense of *spirit* that we may appropriately link morale with childhood.

Morale, basically, is the level of moral-ethical courage at which we make our response to the demands of daily life. It rises and falls like mercury in a thermometer. Each of us has had the experience of a lift in morale through such simple things as a sunny morning, a friendly greeting, a strain of music, a letter from a friend. And each of us has suffered a loss of morale through misunderstanding, sharp words given or received, loneliness, dreary surroundings.

Little children are more vulnerable than grown-ups because they are more tender in all ways and have fewer protective resources. They arrive at their moral-ethical values through the experiences they have in the social world. Morale, or the spirit with which they meet their "life-tasks" is steadily strengthened or undermined by the treatment they receive in the family, the school, the community. Where does good morale come from? Perhaps it has three sources—secure and satisfying human relations early in life; positive use of power; adequacy in the world outside the home.

Secure and satisfying human relations: Does it seem fantastic to suggest that a child's morale is related to his parents' feelings about him before he is born? The balance is on his side, truly, if he was really wanted, and wanted so much that he did not have to compete with economic security or established social status for his existence. There is nothing that sets a baby up like being wanted. It gives him the edge on all the rest of the world, because if he is wanted the chances are that he will be deeply and warmly loved, and if he is loved the chances are that he will like himself and other people. It is like a snowball, the cumulative benefit of being wanted.

Morale is nourished if he is really a part of the family. In too many homes there is a wall between adults and children. The feeling exists that children live in one world and grown-ups in another. Parents in such homes often struggle and sacrifice to give their children rich material gifts, and relieve them of all hardship and responsibility. This is a questionable good. No matter how materially abundant a child's life is, it just isn't good enough. The child who is shut out of the struggle and sacrifice, not included in the purposes, admitted only to the easy and pleasant things, is a deprived child. Secure and satisfying family life depends on really belonging to the family.

Positive use of power: With all of us morale depends to some degree on our being able to control something. Many of the problems of adult relationship which baffle us today, and many of the behavior problems of children and adolescents grow out of a deep, natural need for power and a restless search for fulfillment of the need. Perhaps in no other aspect of life do children need more help and guidance than in the understanding of their own power drives and the constructive satisfaction of them.

It is not power, in itself, which is dangerous to individuals and societies, but the ways in which power is used and expressed. A considerable part of the fantasy life of young children has to do with power. We see it reflected in the popularity of certain kinds of play equipment and paraphernalia, in the language and gesture children use among themselves. It is when power comes to be confused with force that trouble begins in any social group.

Just as good morale comes from being wanted, from being "in" on family life early, from learning early to share life with other people, so too it comes from having a place to play, things to play with, children to play with. It comes from learning how to order raw materials into a creative design, from building with blocks, painting, working with clay, with wood and tools, with earth and water and all the plastic malleable materials possible. It comes from reading, from knowing the power and beauty of words as they are organized around ideas.

Adequacy in the world outside the home: And finally, morale depends on the picture of himself which the child builds as he goes out into the world. School experience is profoundly important to morale. For many children the first grade is either an opening or a closing door, according to the understandings, perception and practices in human relations which interleave the primers and workbooks. The first grade—a composite of loose teeth, knobby knees, chapped hands, runny noses, strange language, noise, aggression, eagerness for new experience, anxiety, vulnerability—is a wellspring or a desert so far as the morale of a large number of our children is concerned. And from it the rest of the society derives part of its own spirit. For from the first grade, ideas, aspirations, patterns of relationship flow back into the homes and the communities, and feed those values by which men live—"the rational and humane values which are inseparable from democracy if it is to be of any worth."

TIME

Time has no divisions to mark its passage, there is never a thunderstorm or blare of trumpets to announce the beginning of a new month or year. Even when a new century begins it is only we mortals who ring bells and fire off pistols.—Thomas Mann.

Kids in the Kitchen

By MARGUERITA RUDOLPH

There is no other single activity so universally appealing and rewarding to all children as cooking. Sometimes "cooking" may be only elementary help on the part of the small child, or it may be a teen-ager's proud production of an elaborate angel food cake. In either case the cooking is an expression of the child's impulse to take part in a basic family function, to make a personal contribution to it; and in either case, the child takes pleasure in saying, or implying, "I did this."

The child's chief reward from cooking is to see what he or she had personally prepared, eaten and enjoyed (or at least appreciated) especially by grownups. A solid sense of relationship is felt in that. When baby Nina, a year and a half old, breaks off a piece of toast and offers it to Mother, and even places it in her mouth—the act has a sense of contribution and partnership. The

baby under two who is so often under-foot in the kitchen, can be given pots and spoons and even spillable matter to manipulate. In this simple manipulation the baby develops curiosity, control and coordination; he gains an awareness of work and of tools and enjoys a feeling of being occupied on the same plane as the adult human in the kitchen. Even for a baby, life is much richer this way than being constantly excluded and forever kept clean.

A small child of two and three has a great deal of practical knowledge about where things are and should be in the kitchen and he has knowledge of the particular processes in preparing food. He gains this knowledge from keen observation and from occasional participation.

"This is where the frying pan goes, and you have to beat up the egg with the milk, before dumping it out," explained three-year-old Herbie to a newcomer. He watched the lighting of the fire, blew out the match and made sure of its proper disposal. After beating up the egg himself, he also pointed out which were the proper supper dishes. Although Herbie is a so-called delicate, nibbly eater, his table behavior is that of a joyous participant.

Two-year-old Lorraine with her imitative, repetitious, yet so independent manner, comes to you at once, beaming, when you say, "Let's find something to eat." Here is a bag full of groceries and Lorraine takes them all out—some twenty items— one by one, all apparently familiar shapes of packages and familiar colors of wrappings. Touching and smelling it, she puts the bacon in the ice box; pecking with her finger and squeezing with both hands, she places the lettuce in a compartment and puts the lid on. She rummages deep in the bag and fishes out several soup cans, shaking each one gleefully and saying each time "Chicken soup for Lorraine" in her own language, as she places all the cans in a row. She pokes her finger in the cream cheese and licks it, and pronounces it "yum-yum." What a rich experience in the touching and the shaking and the smelling for a two-year-old; what an opportunity to gain a lusty appreciation of food!

Preschool children have an insatiable curiosity about everything, which shows their eagerness to learn, their natural intelligence. This curiosity is particularly active and particularly fresh and challenging to adults, when it comes to food and the doings in the kitchen. Ordinary, everyday-ish, even tiresome things in the kitchen appear fresh and fascinating and fun to young children. Milk — bubbling, brimming and finally boiling over—is very interesting; a heaping pot of vigorous look-ing spinach that limps and dimin-ishes and practically vanishes in cooking is so fascinating that it makes four-year-old Mary exclaim suspiciously to mother: "Did you take that spinach away while I wasn't looking?" "Then *where* did it go?" She wonders, and watches and wants an answer. In getting an answer she is still skeptical and she wants "to see" again and again. She may be getting in the way of the scheduled and automatic adult, but she is sens-ing from the sight of the mere spinach the relation between solids and liquids, the powerful action of heat, and the drama of physical transformation.

Success

There are many kinds of success in life worth having. It is exceedingly interesting and attractive to be a successful business man, a railway man, a farmer, or a successful lawyer or doctor; or a writer, or a President, or a ranchman, or the colonel of a fighting regiment, or to kill grizzly bears and lions. But for the unflagging interest and enjoyment, a household of children, if things go reason-ably well, certainly makes all other forms of success and achieve-ment lose their importance by comparison.

—*Theodore Roosevelt*

Learning To Control Emotions

By RHODA W. BACMEISTER

"Oh, you naughty girl!" Vera Blake scolded. "You've been as cross as two sticks all day. Now you just *stop* it!"

Before Vera's angry voice little Kathy's scowl gave way to wide-eyed alarm, then a burst of tears, "But Mummie" she choked, "I don't *like* to be cross. I just *feel* that way!"

Repentantly Vera swept the child up into her arms, "There, honey don't cry. I guess I was being cross, too, and neither of us wanted to. We all get that way sometimes." By recognizing honestly that our emotions are not usually intentional she was helping Kathy take a first step toward controlling her emotions.

Nobody says to himself, "Now I think I'd better get furiously angry (or be ashamed, or fall in love)" and then proceeds to do it. Emotions just *happen* to us. They are nothing to conceal or feel ashamed of, but we can't be blindly ruled by them. It is a long time before we begin to recognize them as they begin to build up

Edward Lettau

and longer still before we are able to control them.

A small child is swept hither and yon by his own unforeseen emotions as helpless as a teen-ager in love. The less sure he is of himself and his place in the family and the larger world about him, the more easily the winds of emotion drive him before them.

Therefore, the first step toward control lies in developing his sense of belonging, of being firmly rooted. This feeling comes to a child in many ways but first through the *dependable* love and trust of his parents. He must know that we love him and have faith in him *all the time.* He is going to get into mischief sometimes and is going to have ugly feelings and behave badly sometimes. These human and ugly thoughts come to all of us.

We will control his actions if necessary and help him learn to control them himself. But we won't ever call him bad and withdraw our love because he misbehaves. This would be to leave him without our support just when he is most threatened by emotional disaster.

Admit and accept your child's emotions without blame. Stand on his side as he learns to control them. Then you don't force him to deny or hide them. It's not safe to cork up lively emotions. Unless they find outlets they form festering sores.

Help your child to find acceptable outlets. Charlie's block tower has toppled again and he is suddenly enraged. Seizing a block, he is about to let fly, regardless of windows or mirrors. You'll have to catch his hand, but you can temper your taboo of

84

this violence by saying, "I know just how you feel. Sometimes I get mad enough to throw things, too, but we can't have the living room smashed up. I know! Let's hammer a while. You can bang nails as hard as you like."

Children can learn to work off ill temper through violent activity, running, climbing, games, and so on. They find out, too, that all kinds of art expressions—music, painting, clay-work, etc. can be used as safety valves. They can boss the dog, spank the dolls, and make up "pretend" situations that give them excuses for free expression of all sorts of feelings. All these help release emotions. They help children understand and face unreasoning fears, and so on.

As the children grow they become more and more capable, independent, and self-confident. Encourage it, for every step along that path increases their self-control and sense of responsibility. Show them how to recognize their own mounting irritability and deal with it before it gets out of hand. Maybe hunger is causing it, or fatigue. Mothers realize that children can learn to. Maybe a change of occupation or companions, or a little time to be alone would straighten the whole thing out. Help your child realize these things and use them to keep pleasant.

But don't set over-high standards or expect *uninterrupted* progress. One gets tense and "tantrumy" from trying to live up to excessive demands. Failure brings a sense of guilt and unhappiness, maybe resentment. It is wise just to let the children know that you expect them to *try,* that you rejoice with them when they succeed and will help, not blame, them if they seem about to fail. For their own sakes as well as that of others, we must prevent acts that would later burden the children with guilt and shame. We must stop bad emotional outlets and provide good ones until the child learns to do it himself.

Here, as elsewhere, example is a powerful teacher. Do we keep our own tempers under control? A child who sees Mother win by tears and Father by shouting and slamming doors would be a fool not to try these methods. Of course, mere human parents will get ill-tempered at times, but they should know better than to explode before the children. As adults we do know various ways to work ourselves out of bad moods. Meantime, it helps our children to see that we, too, have the problem they know so well — and that we know some answers to it!

"Oh, dear!" you may say, "That made me so angry that I'm all snarly inside. I guess I'll go work in the garden a while." Or, "I feel just as bad about having the rain spoil our plans as you do. We'll just have to find some way to cheer ourselves up, won't we?"

At first children are helpless victims of their own emotions. But as they grow they realize that they need not be. Control grows with their experience of being happy and pleasant most of the time. Avoidance of violent situations, clashes, tantrums, etc., is one way we can train for control. Gradually, with your help, the children can learn how to avoid many emotional storms, how to get along with people, how to face failure, disappointment, and so on. Even when thoroughly aroused they will know which outlets are permissible, which taboo. And they will have at their command a number of devices for working themselves out of black moods. That is good equipment for the long struggle toward mature control.

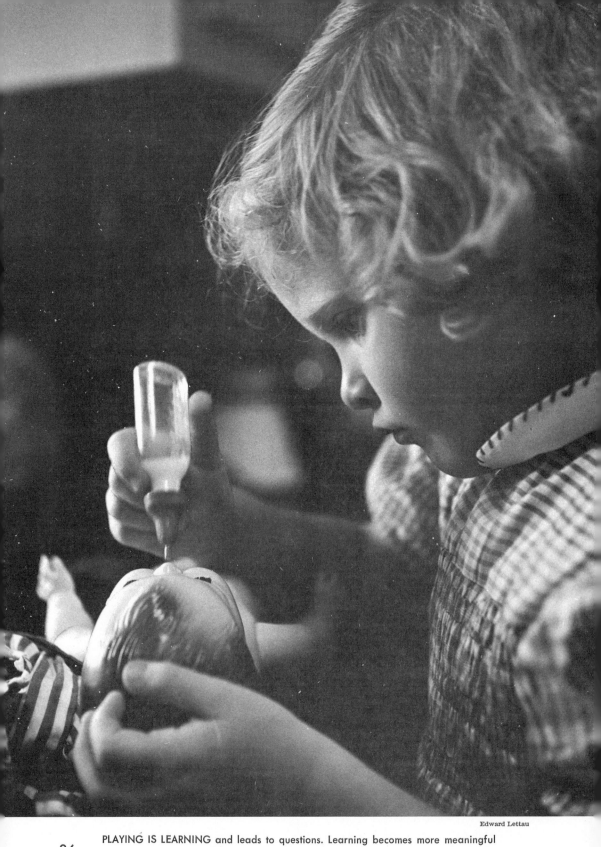

Edward Lettau

PLAYING IS LEARNING and leads to questions. Learning becomes more meaningful
if you answer your child's questions.

Play — Language of Childhood

By BETTYE M. CALDWELL

Despite the casual and carefree appearance which a child's play may have, it is basic to his growth and development and to his ever-emerging understanding of the people and events around him. Play provides a means of self-expression for the child, and by observation of his play we can gain considerable insight into his predominant inner needs.

Perhaps it would be worthwhile to examine and illustrate some of the functions of play activities, an awareness of which would aid parents in understanding their children.

(1) *Play assists the child in the process of assimilating and incorporating experiences.* So full of new experiences is the child's world that he must constantly rearrange old events and ideas in order to make room for newer ones which are clamoring for recognition. Witness a group of children "playing school," or one child putting her dolls through a schoolroom session. Here will stand out in bold relief the attitudes of the

H. Armstrong Roberts

child toward this event—his conception of what a teacher does and how she will react to her pupils, his view of the way children are expected to act, or his feeling about the way they should be permitted to behave. Such play sequences are definitely helpful to the child in coming to the realization that this is another experience which will have meaning in his daily existence.

(2) *Play brings to light conflicts, fears, and anxieties.* Although children are less hesitant than adults to talk openly about those things which make them fearful, they develop at a very early age the feeling that they should not be "sissies" and be afraid of anything and will therefore conceal or disguise the object of their fear. Invariably such dreaded objects will appear in their play, though in a variety of forms. Recently a five-year-old girl went through a phase of playing "doctor" all the time, introducing the theme into every play session with her friends. Also, it was observed that she always insisted upon being the doctor, never willing to take a turn at being the patient. When taken for a routine visit to the doctor, however, her behavior was quite different. Though not overtly appearing fearful, she would say little or nothing to him and rejected in a hostile fashion his attempts to make friends with her. It was later revealed by the mother that the child had had polio the previous summer and had been isolated in the hospital for some time without even being permitted to see her mother. In her play she was acting out her fear of the total situation of being ill, being separated, and of being given injections and other

87

painful treatments by the doctors. Her technique, however, was to attempt to overcome the fear by actually becoming the doctor in the play situation, thereby destroying his ability to incite fear.

(3) *Play provides compensation for defeats, frustrations, and sufferings.* In this area fantasy provides for all of us a very valuable outlet for our feelings. Although an over-abundance of fantasy behavior is not regarded as healthy for adults, it provides children with a source of reward which reality can seldom offer. For example, the small, underweight child can be the strong, husky cowboy in his play. The plain or homely little girl can be a princess or a movie star or anything else she wishes. The healthy child will gradually relinquish this sort of behavior as he learns to make the most of his own resources and accept the limitations imposed by the real world around him, but his play activities provide a means of gratification while this greater stability is emerging.

(4) *Play gives the child a sense of mastery over the environment.* The acquisition of skills required by certain toys or games—riding a bike, throwing and catching a ball, hopping on one foot—give a young child a sense of control over an environment which seems always to be controlling him in one fashion or another. These skills are important for his adaptation to other children and provide valuable techniques for getting along with them.

(5) *Play is instrumental in developing certain social standards.* This is a function of play that is often overlooked, although it is a crucial one indeed. While the play of a very young child is often egocentric and unconcerned with the wishes and desires of others, this condition cannot prevail long. Group play is a social enterprise, a perfect laboratory for learning such essentials as respecting the rights of others and subordinating one's own desires to those of the whole group. And furthermore, on a larger scale, the standards of a society are repeatedly acted out in play, thus enabling a child to gain an understanding of them. To illustrate, the current cowboy craze depicts a constant struggle between the "good" and the "bad," with the good cowboy being visualized as one who is helpful to others and opposed to lawlessness, greed, and unwarranted violence. Through such episodes, in the play which adults often consider a waste of time, the child learns the meaning of such abstract ideas and begins the process of transferring their meaning into life as a whole.

(6) *Play reveals personality traits in the process of becoming crystallized.* There is no better way to observe your child's reaction to contemporaries and their opinion of him, than by watching them at play. Many traits that will be of cardinal importance in his life adjustment will manifest themselves here. Must he always win? Is he willing to take turns? Is he afraid to attempt new experiences? Is he able to be both a leader and a follower? These are questions deserving of careful thought and consideration by everyone concerned with guiding and teaching children.

It is worth saying, in summary, that play provides a method whereby a child can share himself with other people and other objects in his environment. Through this medium he re-enacts, relives, and re-creates many experiences which are meaningful to him. It is truly a crystal ball into which parents may gaze and see reflected those aspects of life which are most important to their child. Gaze often and you will find an open sesame into your child's world.

What Would You Do About
A FRIGHTENED CHILD?

By RALPH K. MEISTER

FATHER DISCOVERS some scratches and gouges on the hallway wall. Strongly suspecting this to be the work of son Robert, age four, he bellows for the presumptive culprit to appear on the scene. Robert begins crying even before he arrives. He steadfastly maintains his innocence, even though Father finally promises not to punish him if he will tell the truth.

What would you do?

(a) Believe Robert's story since you have only circumstantial evidence.

(b) Point out that neither you nor his mother did it, which leaves only him.

(c) Punish him doubly for lying.

(d) Calm down, relax and drop the incident until both parties are less upset.

(e) Make Robert remain on the scene until he decides to confess.

Discussion

We may be able to remember our own childhood fairy stories about powerful giants and wicked dragons, and chill at the recollection. Because he isn't breathing fire and smoke, Father when excessively angry may not be confused with a wicked dragon. However, his anger does not remove him too far from the category of a threatening giant. Under the circumstances, because the consequences seem so frightening, a four-year-old could hardly be persuaded to "tell the truth." Unreasoning fear immobilizes him and impels him to protest his innocence against all odds. Therefore, the recommended procedure is (d). (a) and (c) both represent undesirable extremes. If one had to choose one of these two, (a), despite representing an easy out for Robert, is far better than (c). (e) would simply be excessive pressure and might increase Robert's upset state. (b) probably is excellent courtroom procedure but is hardly appropriate for a scared four-year-old.

By all means, if we hope to encourage truthfulness in the very young child, we must not make its consequences too frightening. Excessive anger only makes the child cling more tenaciously to his story, however weak it is.

What Would You Do About
A BUDDING MICHELANGELO?

By RALPH K. MEISTER

GREGORY, age four, has just submitted to father a drawing purporting to be a likeness of his mother. It is a roughly egg-shaped figure with eyes, nose and mouth; arms project out from the side of the egg and two legs are attached to the bottom edge. A swirl of green hair tops off the production.

What would you do?

(A) MAKE A MENTAL NOTE that an art career for Gregory is out of the question.

(B) ASK MOTHER when she dyed her hair green.

(C) TELL GREGORY as charitably as you can that it is all right.

(D) CALL MOTHER IN TO SEE it and praise Gregory liberally.

(E) HANG IT UP in his room or your room for awhile.

(F) TRY TO POINT OUT to Gregory that while it is a good try, it doesn't, for instance, have a neck or separate trunk.

Discussion

The young child's self-confidence and motivation is rather closely tied up with what his parents think of what he does. Therefore, (D) and (E) are recommended if we want to encourage Gregory's further efforts and develop his feeling of self-confidence. Actually because his drawing is very good for his age, (A) would be a poor and premature judgment. (B) is the kind of raillery the child cannot appreciate but which he may sense as depreciating. (C) also is basically depreciating. (F) is a response that expects too much of a child at this time, burdens him with perception of details he will automatically learn as he grows older. (E) is especially recommended because it gives the child serious, demonstrated recognition as well as verbal approval.

What Would You Do About
TOO MUCH CANDY?

By RALPH K. MEISTER

Robert, age 4, got into a large box of his mother's candy and was not discovered until he had overstuffed himself to the point where he was actually sick. Now he is crying and wailing that his stomach hurts.

If you were Robert's parents, what would YOU do?

a. Offer him some more candy.

b. Insist that he eat the pieces he has bitten into so that this will really be a good lesson to him.

c. Deny him any candy for the next month.

d. Let him know in so many words that you think he has made a pig of himself and that this serves him right.

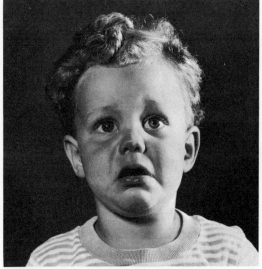

Constance Bannister

e. Check his regular candy allotment to see if it seems adequate to satisfy his routine craving for sweets.

f. Give him something to ease his pain and put him to bed.

Discussion

"A" and "B" would be questionable procedures because, to the extent that unpleasant consequences are instructive, Robert has "learned his lesson." "D" might represent your true feelings but would undoubtedly seem unsympathetic to Robert and might provoke more insistent wailing. "C" would be punishing but not necessarily effective educationally and would build up a craving that might precipitate another such crisis. "F" would be the best immediate measure, and "E" should be investigated to rule out the possibility that his diet is building up an excessive craving. Incidentally, it might be advised to keep candy out of reach of an easily tempted four-year-old.

What Would You Do About
TATTLING?

By RALPH K. MEISTER

Marcia has developed the habit of tattling on the activities of her younger sister, Linda.

If you were Marcia's parents, what would YOU do?

a. Punish Marcia when she tattles.

b. Point out to her that it is not nice to tattle.

c. Hear her story but do nothing about it.

d. Call Linda to you and settle the issue that was raised.

e. Tell Marcia that you know about what Linda is doing and that it is perfectly all right.

Edward Lettau

f. Send Marcia back to play, gently but firmly.

Discussion

This quiz assumes that there is no strong jealousy or hostility existing between the children. If there were, Marcia's tattling would be direct expression of retaliation against the favoritism she felt her sister was enjoying and would require more extended handling aimed at dissipating the strong feeling of jealousy. However, if this tattling is simply behavior previously encouraged by the amount of attention it secured for Marcia, a combination of (f) and (b) would probably be most effective. Punishment, response (a), would not be fair to Marcia and might elicit another kind of equally undesirable behavior. Response (d) would provide a strong encouragement for further tattling and even (c) is undesirable since listening to the story suggests a certain amount of parental approval. Tattling makes for poor relationship between the children and should generally elicit disapproval. Response (e) is especially poor because it will backfire on the parent not only in approving possible misbehavior on Linda's part but also in setting an undesirable precedent. The next time Marcia does the same thing she will undoubtedly remember that you said it was all right for Linda to do it.

What Would You Do About
THE CHILD WHO WON'T EAT?

By RALPH K. MEISTER

Gerald, age four, was not permitted to have his dessert until he had finished all of the food on his plate. This worked for a while, except for his begging and wheedling, but lately he has hardly been eating at all, in spite of the incentive of his dessert.

If you were Gerald's parents, what would YOU do?

a. Cut out any candy, sweets or other treats until he resumes regular eating.

b. Tell him he is a "big boy" now and he will not have to clear his plate in order to have his dessert; when he feels he does not want any more of the other foods, then he can have his dessert.

c. Have him remain at the table until everyone else is finished so he will come to realize that his behavior merely cuts down on his evening play time.

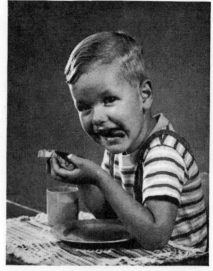

Photograph by Harold M. Lambert

d. Put his dessert away for him and make it a bedtime snack.

e. Make him some additional promises, such as a small toy each week, if during that week he eats well.

Discussion

This month's quiz is an attempt to illustrate the well-recognized fact that children's eating problems do not arise spontaneously but, more typically, are created by parental over-concern. Therefore, (e) would be an especially poor response since it would be an even more obvious attempt to bribe the child to eat and he would use this situation for gaining greater concessions. Responses (a) and (c) have a flavor of punishment about them and would very likely be so interpreted by the child and therefore these methods might well engender a strong resistance to eating. Of course, if the child has been having too many between-meal snacks, these definitely should be cut down but not in a spirit of punishment. Response (b) would probably furnish the best long-run approach to the problem. The first week or so Gerald might "abuse" the new order by concentrating on dessert but very soon in the absence of any outside pressure his normal appetite would insure his getting a well-rounded meal. Response (d) is neither particularly bad nor particularly good. It simply does nothing about the problem.

What Would You Do About
DAWDLING AT BEDTIME?

By RALPH K. MEISTER

Peter is now more than half an hour late for his bedtime and while having his hands and face washed by his mother is making dirt designs on the sink with his free and as yet unwashed hand, calling mother's attention to this informal finger-painting achievement.

If you were Peter's mother, what would YOU do?

(a) Lecture him for being a bad boy for making a mess of the sink and further delaying his bedtime.

(b) Simply admonish him to quit such puttering.

(c) Insist that he wash himself and report to you afterwards.

(d) Note what he is doing, even admire it, but do not let this distract you from the main job of getting

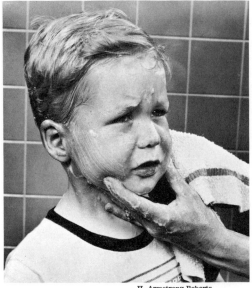

H. Armstrong Roberts

him finished with as much dispatch as possible.

(e) Start washing both hands at once to stop the additional messing.

Discussion

The particular example chosen is but one of many devices which children of this age adopt, not necessarily with malice aforethought or to thwart a beleaguered parent but because this is the kind of inventive game which often genuinely fascinates them. At this stage of the evening, (d) or (e) look like good bets depending upon your mood. Peter can hardly be held responsible for getting to bed on time, so if he is late you are at least partly to blame if only for your failure to follow through. Therefore (a) is not desirable. (c) is inadvisable because training in self-help should not be made in a punitive context. (b) is all right if Peter goes along but it is likely to raise a disciplinary issue which can lead to a frayed temper for mother and tears for Peter. The problem is intended to help avoid the parental stringency and sharpness that sometimes result in such situations. Moral: Begin preparing Peter for bed in enough time so that his inevitable dawdling will not disorganize either of you.

What Would You Do About
A PARENTAL MISTAKE?

By RALPH K. MEISTER

Father, repairing a chair, found his tube of glue missing. He has just finished scolding Gerald, age four, for having used the tube to paste pictures in his scrapbook. Now, mother has come on the scene and reports that she gave Gerald permission to use the glue because she had forgotten to get him the regular paste on her shopping trip as she had promised to do.

If you were Gerald's father, what would YOU do?

(a) Remonstrate with mother for having given him the permission.

(b) Let the matter drop after impressing upon Gerald that he is not in the future to use glue for this purpose.

(c) Insist that the money for the paste now be used to replace the tube of glue.

(d) Apologize to Gerald for having mistakenly blamed him for wrong doing.

Discussion

This is one of those instances where father's irritation may be sufficiently general to have him do the wrong thing. If he is going to remonstrate with mother (a), he had better do that later and preferably in privacy. However, the only acceptable handling of the mistake is alternative (d). We parents should never feel that the respect of our children depends upon our being always right. We do make mistakes and we put the respect our children have for us on a more solid basis when we honestly admit these. We may be able to bluff Gerald at four by using alternatives (b) or (c) but even then we will not have assuaged Gerald's possible hurt and sense of injustice. But when he is eight we will no longer be able even to bluff him and will in the meantime have substantially damaged the child's sense of respect for us and the large measure of security which he derives from being able to respect us. So, go on — apologize.

What Would You Do About
THE CHILD WHO SLAPPED MOTHER?

By RALPH K. MEISTER

Kathy, age 4, slipped and fell and although comforted seemed to cry all out of proportion to her injury. So Mother called her a "cry baby." Kathy said, *"I am not,"* and Mother said, *"You are, too!"* After a few repetitions of the "I am not — you are too" routine, Kathy slapped at her mother's face.

If you were Kathy's mother, what would YOU do?

(a) Slap Kathy's hand because no child should ever strike a parent.

(b) Act injured to impress upon Kathy that you are hurt so she won't again strike in anger.

(c) Send Kathy to her room or an isolation corner.

(d) Tell Kathy that besides being a "cry baby," she is a bad girl, too, for slapping her mother.

(e) Take Kathy aside and tell her you are sorry you teased her but that she shouldn't slap her parents.

H. Armstrong Roberts

Discussion

The situation depicted here represents an abuse of parental authority. Actually, mother has teased Kathy beyond the four-year-old's emotional endurance. A temper tantrum might have been an equally disturbing but more socially approved reaction on Kathy's part. Alternative (d) would make bad matters worse. Alternative (b) is particularly bad because it would burden Kathy with a feeling of guilt that is unjustified. Alternative (a) also ignores mother's considerable responsibility for the entire affair. (c) is acceptable if it is used to allow a cooling of tempers on both sides and is followed up with attempts at reconciliation. (e) however, seems most acceptable to this writer. We should not push children beyond their limits of endurance and when we do we should take the initiative for patching up matters.

What Would You Do About
THE FINGER MARKS ON THE CAKE?

By RALPH K. MEISTER

M OTHER BAKED a particularly impressive cake with white frosting only to find it before dinner gouged with finger marks, too indistinct to enable her to identify the culprit as either Nancy, age seven; Ruth, age six; or Terry, age four and a half. Baby Robert, age three months, is obviously ineligible. Mother is understandably irritated.

What would you do?

(a) Make all three sit in chairs until one of them has confessed.

(b) Deny all three any of the cake unless one of them confesses.

(c) Promise that the guilty party would not be punished.

(d) Refuse to bake any more pretty cakes if they are so unappreciated.

(e) Spank all three unless the culprit is revealed.

(f) Lecture them all individually.

Discussion

Alternatives (a), (b), (d), and (e) have in common the fact that the innocent are punished along with the guilty, which is undesirable. It would be far better to drop the matter than to seek to punish the guilty at the cost of also implicating the innocent. Alternative (f) is subject to the same objection since two of the individuals would be getting a lecture which they did not in fact deserve; it might, even more than the others, leave them with the feeling they were unjustly treated. (c) is probably the best bet, not because it solves the problem, but rather because it puts Mother in a position to be able to handle the problem; if she knew who had done it, she would have some notions of why it had been done. The reasons probably would be somewhat different in each of the three possible cases. It should be stressed that the most important consideration is that we learn why this was done in order to deal with the problem of the child, rather than the problem of the maltreated cake.

Oh yes, my own personal guess, if this were a mystery story, is that the culprit is Terry who would be most likely to be jealous of the new baby who had replaced him in the "baby" spot in the family. Recommendation: firm but understanding and sympathetic handling of the culprit when finally discovered.

What Would You Do About

THE CHILD WHO WANTS TO EAT BABY FOOD?

By RALPH K. MEISTER

Bernard, age four-and-a-half, approaches his mother who is feeding his five-month-old sister baby-cereal and asks to have some.

If you were Bernard's mother, what would YOU do?

(a) Refuse him, pointing out very kindly that this is the baby's food.

(b) Offer to hold him in your lap and feed him as soon as you are finished with the baby.

(c) Let him stand by and give him every second spoonful.

Photograph by Harold M. Lambert

(d) Point out that he is a big boy and it is babyish for him to want baby food.

(e) Let him taste some and then offer to prepare a regular dish for him.

Discussion

Enough has been written about possible jealousy toward a new baby in the family to indicate that in our handling of an older child we should strive to avoid giving him any basis for feeling that the baby is especially privileged. This consideration would rule out alternative (a). On the other hand we do not wish to encourage babyishness in Bernard so (b) would be inappropriate. (d) is inappropriate because it seeks to suppress Bernard's desire without doing anything about it and uses shaming, which is generally an undesirable method of handling a situation. (c) constitutes the kind of acquiescing compromise which seems to encourage competition. It seems inadvisable, too, because it is messy and interferes with the baby's feeding. (e) would be the desirable alternative. It does not deny Bernard his request yet is sufficiently matter-of-fact so that Bernard will be very likely to drop the entire issue after the first time. And if he does not? There is nothing in baby-cereal that is harmful to a four-year-old nor is it so expensive that Bernard could not have a dish of it daily.

IV

What Are Growth Standards For?

By RHODA W. BACMEISTER

Do you worry if your child is small for his age or hasn't learned to read by seven? Do you brag if he is ahead of his age in school or plays ball better than the other ten-year-olds? It's very natural to feel that way, and sometimes wholesome, but sometimes it can make trouble for parents and children.

We do more of such comparing of children's development than our grandparents did because some years ago it occurred to scientists that to guide our children wisely we probably needed to know more about normal growth patterns and rates. Thereupon a wave of testing and measuring children swept over the country and suddenly we learned an awful lot about the growth of the non-existent *average* American child.

As this information got passed down from laboratories to homes and schools, little Johnny Jones and Mary Brown were carefully compared with this fictitious child. Was he, or she, "up to average" or better, in size, in spelling, in social development—and if not how could we make him so?

Of course, practically nobody fitted the pattern. Our children, thank Heaven, are not standardized, mass-produced products. They are as wonderfully varied as they should be in a society based on the right of every individual to be himself . . . the scientists realized that. They knew that some children grow fast, some slowly, and some by spurts, that the same child may do all three in different respects, and that this is normal.

Unfortunately this feeling of the wide range of normal individual differences was not as easy to pass on as the tables of averages. It took much

longer to get into the homes, and meantime a lot of unlucky children were pushed and prodded to develop in ways or at speeds not natural to them. Sometimes it was in an effort to pull them up to the average; sometimes because a child was superior in some way he was urged on to become a genius. You know our American tendency to competition! "Bigger, or faster, must be better," we seem to think.

But rapid growth is not always a good thing. A gardener knows that the tallest seedlings may not be as strong and healthy as those with slower, well-balanced growth. And just stop and think—how many famous infant prodigies can you remember hearing of? And where are

H. Armstrong Roberts

they now? Not among the leaders in their country, I'll wager!

What are standards good for, then? Obviously they are useful to people who plan for many children. Educators have to know, for example, which books the average nine-year-old can read and will like. Then they can suit most of the children. The teacher will still have to adapt the work to some individual differences.

Parents, too, find averages and age-level standards useful if they will remember the warning that good books in the field usually carry—that averages are not patterns to be copied or records to be beaten, but only examples of what is common at a given age. Any individual parent brings up so few children these days that she can't generalize safely from her own experience, yet it is a comfort to know approximately what to expect.

Mrs. Parks, for instance, was much disturbed when Frances, at five, began to tell fantastic tales as truth. Tommy had never done anything like that; Tommy was practical and literal-minded. But on looking it up she found that a great many five-year-olds act like Frances and get over it by six if well handled. That was a consolation to her. She needn't worry after all.

The way our children keep passing from one stage of development to the next is very disconcerting. We just about learn to manage one kind of behavior when it disappears and up pops something else! It is a real help, therefore, to be able to read up a bit and have an idea what to expect. For there *is* a general growth pattern or sequence which most children follow, *at their own pace and with individual variations.* After Peter's passion for collecting miscellaneous junk (whether at six or eight), will probably come more specialized and organized collecting.

We don't want everybody forced into the same mold, but thoroughly lop-sided people are not usually happy and effective either, so if a child is *too far* from the average we look for the reason. There may be some difficulty, physical, mental, emotional, or one of opportunity and circumstance. We may decide there is no need to do anything. Or perhaps Anne needs glasses to help her catch up with her schoolwork. Possibly Jeffrey should be interested in a canoe trip with other boys so as to broaden him and balance the musical interests that are absorbing him completely.

Yes, growth averages have their uses for parents. They must never be used stiffly and literally as standards to be met or surpassed. That means useless worry for parents and harmful pushing and warping of children. But they can be used to help us understand our children better, to have an idea of the usual sequence of growth phases so that we are less perplexed by the kaleidoscope of development. They help us to see each child's unique excellencies and problems, the places where he needs special opportunities or special help. They show us where we might offer chances for more balanced growth and let the child use them as he may, keeping his inalienable right to be *himself*.

THE RIGHT APPROACH

A teacher was spending the vacation taking care of her sister's children while the sister was in the hospital. For several days the six-year-old took part in the efficient program of sharing the daily chores that she had outlined for the youngsters. Then finally he balked. "Aunt Amy," he said, tugging on her skirts, "Aunt Amy, Mummy *lets* me help with the dishes. You *make* me."

—Journal of Education

The Meaning of "Thank You"

By MARGUERITA RUDOLPH

ALL CIVILIZED HUMAN BEINGS have socially acceptable ways of expressing gratitude. This expression does not come automatically with age, like new teeth pushing through tender gums. We—parent and teacher—must first give our children healthy *experiences* that promote good feeling. We cannot rely on a constant *say please* or *say thank you* unless we are satisfied with mere word usage by a child. Young children need first to *feel* gratitude before they can understand the meaning of *thank you*. Thankfulness is not just a word. Nursery-school children have taught me this over and over again.

One day, trying to be economical, I cut several sticks of chewing gum in halves to give a treat to the children. Almost every child in the class of five-year-olds asked the reason for the cutting. I told them the supply of gum would go further that way. Each child accepted his small portion with an air of "oh, well—half a stick is better than none." There was practically no show of gratitude.

Barbara was out of the room and had not received her share of the gum when her mother came for her. "But I didn't get mine yet," she complained to her mother. "Oh, `here's your piece," I said, offering Barbara half a stick as I'd done with the other children. Barbara looked slightly scornful but took the gum without a word of complaint or thanks.

"Well, what do you say?" Barbara's mother prompted. Barbara looked up and said seriously and quietly, "I like a whole piece better."

Naturally this was embarrassing to the mother. She threatened to take the gum away unless the child said *thank you* in a proper way.

Barbara's feeling and words proved to be a real lesson to me, a teacher of young children. The economy I was practicing was arbitrary and habitual —there was no real need for it. My rationing of gum was an act of stinginess, and stinginess cannot bring out feelings of appreciation and *meaningful* words of *thank you* from children. The next day I could say to the children, "When we have gum for a treat, everyone gets a whole piece—I have enough now."

"Me, too?" asked Barbara. "Good!"

"Thank you!" shouted another child.

"Tomorrow I'll bring *you* a *whole* package—I'll ask my mother to buy it," said a third child with characteristic childish gratitude and generosity. Then I *knew* that adults first must see that children have something to be *thankful for* before they can expect them to say *thank you* with the nice warm feelings that should go with the phrase.

Children usually are so appreciative and responsive that it is easy to please them—it need not involve expense or elaborateness. I believe, also, that children are not materialistic until they acquire such values from adults. They are far more sensitive to feelings and attitudes than to things which are provided for them.

Once I watched a seven-year-old child in boarding school rather mechanically tear open a dozen birthday packages she had received by mail. Then she sat for a long time in the midst of the profuse and glossy wrappings, playing distractedly with the ribbons. This little girl had received a quantity of impersonal, unrelated *things,* and she reacted accordingly.

But, on the other hand, I have seen a two-year-old show enormous pleasure and appreciation when served special "apple wheels" on a bread board by the hostess of an adult tea party. The hostess even took time to point out the charming design of black seeds in the center of the slices. The child devoured the apple, piece by piece, saying it was *good.* Later, he talked about it at home and thereafter associated the thoughtful hostess with "apple wheels." No expensive or elaborate offering could have compared with that one ordinary apple, given to him with personal interest and generous attention.

Ritual and Pageantry in the Life of a Child

By ARTHUR L. RAUTMAN

What parent has not observed, often with some amusement, the spontaneous rituals of his children? The one-year-old may want to touch the light switch with his outstretched forefinger each time he is carried past it; the four-year-old just *has* to drink out of his blue mug instead of from an ordinary cup; and the eight-year-old walks across the living-room in a zig-zag path in order to follow the pattern on the rug!

Left to their own devices, children tend to develop ritualistic and compulsive behaviors that add little to their personal and social adjustment and happiness. Intelligently developed with help from grown-ups, however, such ritualistic patterns of behavior may come to permeate the central core of family life. They are the endearingly familiar little characteristics which set off *our* family from all others and which make *our* parents and brothers and sisters so especially beloved. The popcorn always made by Dad on Sunday eve-nings, the family dog's exasperating persistence in jumping out of his pen, and even the weekly washing of the family car build vital memories of family living.

Without adult assistance in their recognition, many of the truly significant events of life will pass unidentified and unnoticed, for children have to *learn* to perceive the richness which surrounds them. Even in great holiday celebrations, such as Christmas Day or Thanksgiving, children need help in sensing the true values and emotions underlying what sometimes seems over-commercialism.

We want children to realize that for them, as for us, the throng of passing days is filled both with comfortable, predictable routine *and* with many joyous special events—birthdays, visits, parties, trips, and many small informal celebrations, as well as great "occasions."

And, perhaps even more important, we want our youngsters to realize that in all of these events they can enhance their own perceptiveness and

enjoyment by playing an *active* part. Even as observers they can actively *enjoy* the world around them.

What, then, do we, as adults, remember from our own childhood; and what do we want our children to remember with pleasure and anticipate with joy?

We recall seeing the first robin in the spring—an event that was important because we realized, if only dimly, that it marked the coming of a new growing season and the promise of abundance. We remember finding the first delicate spring flower; we remember sensing the foreboding implicit in the first frost; and we still remember witnessing the breath-taking beauty of the season's first snowfall. Such occasions not only set off the seasons. They sharpened our awareness of our own personal existence and enhanced our appreciation of the world which is our home.

Watching Mother get out the winter clothes from storage, and helping Father put on the storm-windows were special events akin to Christmas and Thanksgiving. The first day of school in the fall, or the community picnic marking the end of the school year—these were landmarks in our lives. These are the kinds of things we want our children to experience and remember and, in their turn, hand on to the next generation.

In these dramatizations of our life-role and of our relationships with others, small events can be as important as great occasions. The evening bedtime story may well be the most important part of the day, in helping the youngster establish meaningful ties with his otherwise busy and preoccupied parents. In holding open the door for his mother a small boy may experience a sense of importance as great as that felt by Sir Walter, romantically spreading his coat for a queen to walk on—and the flourish thus put into a simple task may transform a humdrum world into a universe of chivalry and aspiration.

If the rituals and pageantry of childhood are to have meaning and continuity, however, they must have the sincere encouragement and whole-hearted participation of the adults in the child's life. Some of these special events should have predictable regularity, and all of them must receive from adults the same earnest cooperation which we extend to the projects of friends whose opinions we value highly. The special Sunday morning breakfast need not be an unvarying procedure, of course; but it should be a *dependable* part of regular family living—not merely something that occurs when it happens to suit the convenience of the adults. The child must sense at least a dependable attitude and steady appreciation in his parents — and not find his efforts sometimes applauded and sometimes ridiculed.

The ability to enjoy and appreciate ritual and pageantry is a frame of mind. Through their example and encouragement parents can help their children learn to participate with pleasure in the rituals of our culture and to derive genuine stimulation and reassurance from them. Like our forms of religious observance, our social customs and even the simple common courtesies of daily life, are rituals which can help to make daily living together less drab and more comfortable and productive.

Parents *can* thus help their children to see the pageantry and color which are everywhere present in everyday life — in the seasons, the changes of the hours, and in the human carnival in which all of us unknowingly participate.

H. Armstrong Roberts

Your Child's Friends

By RHODA W. BACMEISTER

One of the most important lessons we all have to learn is how to choose, make, and keep friends. Another is when and how to let them go. One doesn't learn, either, just by being told how. We have to "learn by doing." Children too!

They make a good many mistakes in the process—and learn from them, though not as fast as we wish. They bite and kick, insult and betray their playmates from time to time, and they find out how it feels to be on the receiving end of such behavior, too. They develop tremendous admirations for particular companions, worthy or unworthy. They experiment with "crushes" and jealousy, with the exclusive club, and with the gang organization.

None of this need alarm us. Children need some of these social adventures on a childish level before they encounter them on a bigger scale. They have to find out by experience that friendship is a two-way thing. They never get it unless they

can be kind and friendly, generous and loyal themselves, and not always then.

Meantime we must watch, console when necessary, guide when we can, and help them—so far as they are able, to see the *meaning* of each experience. But we won't say, "I told you so," and we won't try to stop social exploration.

It begins early. A couple of my neighbors had babies the same age and I have enjoyed watching the development of their play together. Before they were a year old Billy and Barbie showed pleasure at being in the same play pen, though they grabbed each other's hair and toes as freely as they did toys. By two they often played side by side, using similar toys, and by three there was genuine play-*together* in the sense of sharing and cooperating.

Naturally there was also much squabbling. I watched that go from wailing at the loss of a toy through fighting for it, "telling mama," smashing things for revenge, and so on. At first the fights were quickly over and forgotten, but later, apologies or other overtures were needed in "making it up." They always did make up though, even after eight-year-old Barbie, head in the air, informed me.... "I'm not speaking to Billy," and went off to play with Vangie, a tough little character from another street.

That worried her mother while it lasted, for Barbie picked up some rough habits and language. But she learned a good deal of self-confidence and independence, too, before they broke up over whether to "hook" apples from a fruit stand. In the end, Becky's mother thought it had been a profitable experience.

"You see, I encouraged them to play *here* rather than on the street so I could keep an eye on them. Vangie was here constantly, using all Becky's things, but I have to admit she had her points. Maybe I've babied Becky too much. She admired Vangie for all the things she could do and the way she'd try anything. But when it came to a showdown, you see, Becky's home standards won. And when she found Vangie had made off with a pair of her hair ribbons, that settled it. I guess we all learned something from the experience."

I quite agree. Mother was wise in accepting Becky's new friend in the home not only to supervise play but because every member of a family should be free to bring his friends home. Vangie probably learned a good deal there, too, which was clear gain. And it was good that Mother could see the virtues that attracted Becky to Vangie.

It's not always easy for us to do that, the compatibility of two people is such an intangible thing. Every child's social needs are as individual as his personality, and change, too, as he grows—and with them his admiration for different kinds of people. Nor are children likely to size people up with the same yardstick adults use. Other things seem important to them.

So it is no use trying to hand-pick our children's friends. We can give them chances to play with children we admire (or whose parents we like) and if they happen to get along, that's fine. But real friendship can no more be forced than love can.

For one thing, it takes time to become a "tried and true" friend, and the long view is hard for children. They are pals today and "mad" tomorrow. They think in terms of good or bad, friend or foe. It's simpler than realizing that we are all good *and* bad, that almost any two people can find ways in which they can cooperate as friends and others on which they must separate. Marriages as well as friendships are wrecked on the rock of "all or nothing."

Children, being human, keep searching for the perfect companion. We can't save them entirely from the resulting disillusionments. But we can soften each blow by showing them the loss is not total. One can set limits and still be friendly within them. Peter may be cruel to animals. One hates that, rejects it, tries to stop it. But Peter is still the best tree-climber on the block. If climbing is the order of the day—come on, Peter!

If we help our children to be friendly, cooperative, loyal, and dependable themselves, they will make friends—all sorts of friends. Perhaps by the time they are grown we can also have taught them tolerance and discrimination. Tolerance is a mature virtue and comes slowly through many experiences in learning to value people in spite of their weaknesses. So the idol has feet of clay— but the rest is pure ivory!

Each of us needs a great many friendly acquaintances, a lot of friends, and a few really dear and close ones. A sincere, friendly person who does not demand perfection can draw friends closer through the years. Or if it seems best to part, he can usually make it drifting apart, not tearing apart explosively. I believe that we can help even children *begin* to understand such things.

Fun with Poetry

By EDITH FORD

Edward Lettau

Between the dark and the daylight
When the night is beginning to lower
Comes a pause in the day's occupation
Which is known as the children's hour.

—Henry Wadsworth Longfellow

A children's hour is definitely a thing which every family would learn to enjoy whether it be that twilight hour when it is too light to turn the bright lights on and too dark to go about real work without them—or perhaps the hour after dinner.

Both hours have points in their favor for an intimate get-together of mother and children, or better still, parents and children. The twilight hour, when night is beginning to draw her curtains around gives a cozy feeling of well being when the big jobs are almost done and the tempo of the day's rush has slowed down a bit.

The hour after dinner brings a satisfied feeling when the last big task is done, when hunger pains have been quelled and all relax for a time, perhaps before an open fire or perhaps in just a warm, cheerful room.

This time has an added allurement in that Father, too, may be a part of this cozy gathering.

Whatever the hour it may well be a sharing time, a time when news of the day may be exchanged, when highlights are recalled for others to enjoy. And sharing times are conducive to gathering such gems along the way as glimpses of a beautiful sky, snatches of a happy song, a flash of a gayly colored dress, or an amusing joke.

After the day's jewels have been pooled, why not share bits of poetry? Here, indeed, lies untold wealth to be had for the asking. Mother and Father may find they have a surprising store from their own childhood. If they have some poetry that is fun, some that is beautiful, the children will not want to be outdone. They too, will want to be contributing members of the group.

Suppose Father and Mother do not quite remember just how any poems go. Why not hunt up some good ones to read? First of all, choose poems that are fun for our lively boys and girls of today. The beautiful ones can come a little later.

Father, *or* perhaps Mother, may enjoy reading "The Pirate Don Dirke of Dowdee" quite as much as their listeners enjoy hearing about this wicked but gorgeous pirate. Particularly will they enjoy reading it if they will just let themselves enter whole-heartedly into the spirit of this rollicking poem. Before anyone knows it the whole family will be chiming in on certain lines whose lilt and musical words jingle quite as much as the pirate's gold.

Why not try Eleanor Farjeon's "The Lady in the Tower"? What happens to a lady locked up in a tower should appeal to any boy and girl. This poem also has some very good jokes hidden away in its lines and an oft-repeated refrain of "Heigh-O-fiddle-de-de." Read this dramatically and before you know it your listeners will pick up your mood with a "Heigh-O-fiddle-de-de."

And if the family really wants some fun together, try Vachel Lindsay's "Daniel." Why not let Father tell the story and then there is a part for everyone? Here is a whole play wrapped up in a poem! The entire family will want to be the lions roaring, "We want Daniel, Daniel, Daniel" as though they were cheering the home team at a football game. Try it and see what fun!

Then there's Laura Richards', "Skinny Mrs. Snipkin" which is fun just to hear or to read, but still more fun if someone tells the story, and one takes the part of the skinny Mrs. Snipkin and another, the part of fat Mrs. Wobble-chin. Or if you like rollicking rhythm there is Miss Richards', "Seven Little Tigers." If someone objects to being a little tiger he can take the part of the aged cook. If you like a good sea story with some right "salty" parts to play, try Thackeray's "Little Billie." Another story poem with plenty of parts to play, a fascinating rhythm, and loads of fun is Milne's "The King's Breakfast." This poor king has such a time just getting a little butter for his bread!

For the more serious moments try reading together "What Does It Mean to be American?", "The Flag Goes By," or "O Captain, My Captain." The possibilities are endless when the family starts enjoying poetry together. Before you know it, you will all be *saying* poems, not *reading* them.

No "Harmless" Fireworks

More lives have been lost in celebrating American independence than in acquiring it. In the Revolutionary War, 4,044 Americans were killed and 6,004 wounded, while in the 30-year period from 1900 to 1930, 4,290 people were killed by fireworks, and 96,000 injured. This did not take into account many deaths occurring later but attributable to Fourth of July celebrations. After a searching investigation, the American Museum of Safety reports that there are no such things as "harmless" fireworks.

—*Sunshine* Magazine

Help Your Child Find the Answers

By EVERETT E. SENTMAN

CURIOSITY didn't actually kill the cat, but it can be painful for parents. Mother, starting a fresh day full of patience and pride in her offspring, often ends it in frazzles after an acute attack of the "why-mommies."

A child who has been taking his vitamins can maintain the cross-examination indefinitely, on subjects as personal as sex and as remote as the stars. He may start out before breakfast and still be loaded for bear in the evening when Father gets home. The form of interrogation merely changes from "Why, Mommy?" to "Why, Daddy?" This may call forth some parental crossfire — "Why don't *you* answer his questions?"— and we are off to a generally grouchy evening. The only answer, it seems, is to let your little question-box have his dinner in front of the television set, and pop him into bed before he can get wound up again. Electronic sedation

is slightly less harmful than barbiturates, and it leaves Mother and Father free to discuss their own, "more important" problems at dinnertime.

The above procedure is almost guaranteed to leave your child baffled and frustrated. If it is repeated often, it may win you a new low rating on your child's Parent Scale, and will certainly dull the edge of his curiosity.

Curiosity is a divine gift. It is the mental hunger which leads the child to adapt himself to life on this planet. If you stimulate (you cannot satisfy) the young child's natural curiosity, you help to develop mental attitudes that will open doors of discovery for him all his life.

"What makes it rain?" "Where did I come from?" "How do trains stay on the track?" "Where is God?" "Why do my fingernails grow?" "What makes the TV go on?" From meteorology to biology to physics to theology to physiology to electronics. There is no limit to a child's range of question-asking. But for most of us parents, there are definite limits to our ability to answer. No parent can possibly be a whiz at everything. For satisfactory answers, we must reach out beyond our personal fund of information.

What can you do when your small son or daughter traps you with a question? This is an especially embarrassing predicament for Father, whose excuse for existence, in childish eyes, is not often as apparent as Mother's. Prestige is involved here. Do you or do you not know the answer?

It takes an extremely artful parent

to evade the question by changing the subject. In fact, there is only one honorable way out of this situation, and it happens that it is also the way that will do you and your child the most good. You say to him "Let's find the answer."

The basic tool for finding answers to questions is the encyclopedia. Just what is an encyclopedia? I have often wished that this storehouse of information had a different name. The word "encyclopedia" too frequently conjures up a mental picture of something written in Greek. This reaction is a hangover from the days when knowledge was jealously guarded by the intellectual "elite corps"— when learning was for the few rather than for all. The encyclopedia of today should be called "Adventure Land" or "Seek and Find" or "Fun with Facts." Like the snap-crackle-pop breakfast food, the modern encyclopedia practically talks to you. It has been transformed into the most usable, the most informative, the most exciting general reference work the family can buy. Parents who remember the dull, dry-as-dust encyclopedia volumes of the past should get acquainted with the easy-reading, brilliantly illustrated, practical encyclopedia of today.

Exploring for facts also calls for having a good dictionary in the house, either the big Webster's or one of the more popular abridged versions. Make sure it has a recent copyright date, for your boy will want to know what a "G" is and what "stapp" means. With encyclopedia and dictionary, the basic reference library should include the Book of your religious faith, preferably an edition which is indexed and annotated.

The dictionary gives your child the meanings of words, the Book of faith stimulates his interest in traditions and precepts of your religious belief, and the encyclopedia tells him the meanings of human knowledge and activity in every conceivable field.

You may add other home reference tools as time goes on. As your child develops special interests and hobbies, specialized books will suggest themselves.

Once established, the urge to explore for information knows no time of day. If you're the kind of parent who insists on rigid time schedules you had better forget the whole matter. Mealtime is a favorite time for question-asking, and many families have placed their encyclopedia in the dining area for ready use. The books may come to bear visible evidences of what you had for dinner, but who cares? Enthusiasm for learning is more important than "keeping the books nice."

With the home reference library installed, we have Father—and Mother, too—off the spot when Bobby or Susan asks a humdinger. There are long-range benefits, too. Children who, with parent guidance, develop the reference-book habit in early childhood gain a priceless advantage in school work. The next step comes when your child learns the alphabet, and with a little gentle encouragement goes to find the volume and even the page of the encyclopedia where the subject in question is discussed. And later, through example and training, he makes that important step from "Why, Mommy?" to "I'll find it myself." And he reads and learns.

The child who never learns to find the answers is only half living; he sees the world dimly. What are your dreams for him? Doctor, lawyer, merchant, chief? These dreams can be fully realized only if you give your child a solid preschool foundation for mental growth, along with his physical, spiritual, and social development.

Developing Your Child's Vocabulary

By ROBERT H. SEASHORE

How can you help your child acquire a larger, more effective vocabulary? A word a day? Perhaps, but how many words, approximately, does your child learn each day without your help? We know that the average increase per year in school is about 5,000 words or 10 to 15 words a day. This increase in total vocabulary includes both *basic* and *derived* words. Basic words are those such as *friend* and *manage*; derived words—*management, friendship* and *friendly*. Since we have a "natural" increase of 10 to 15 words a day, methods such as "a word a day" become a little antiquated—the 365 new words themselves would be "a mere drop in the bucket."

If this is true, must we then look forward to drilling our children on 10 or 15 words a day? We think not; fortunately there are more effective ways of helping our children than through daily drill on memorizing specific words.

Ewing Galloway

Often we say, "Experience is the best teacher," and parents are probably more aware of the wisdom of this statement than any other single group. How many of us, for example, have told a child, "It's hot," only to have the child demonstrate the inadequacy of this learning by touching the stove! Fortunately, most children's experiences are likely to be much pleasanter than this, but the principle of learning by experience still seems to be a very effective method of building vocabulary, and it is something which can be accelerated by giving children many informal opportunities to learn.

An understandable definition of an escalator may soon be forgotten, but what child can forget what an escalator is after experiencing the thrill of his first ride? A shopping expedition with Mother or Father can teach him not only *escalator* but other words such as *counter, floorwalker, manager, clerk, salesgirl, check, elevator, department*, etc., particularly if the parent is aware that learning can and does take place in such a new experience. Trips to the zoo and museums are fun and painless learning devices as well. Even a bus ride can add words to a child's vocabulary, e.g., *fare, motorman, transfer*.

Words gained through new experiences may be lost if they are not made an active part of the child's vocabulary. Children often "activate" newly acquired words by relating their adventures to playmates and other members of the family. Sometimes the experience is relived quite spontaneously through play. Children seem to be proud of their newly acquired skills and use them over and over again. Needless to say, this should be encouraged and aided at the opportune time.

You can help in a more direct manner by using words which he has recently learned in different parts of speech when you are talking with him. For instance, an older child may have learned *manager*. In your conversation you might make a point of using such allied words as *management, to manage, manageable*. In such a way you further broaden the possibilities for learning from new experiences.

Although a trip downtown may produce more *noticeable* increases in your child's vocabulary, your own daily vocabulary is gradually absorbed by the growing child. What your child learns and how much he learns is, then, in a large part dependent on your vocabulary and the use you make of it. More than anything children want to be grown-up and so they imitate you. If you choose your words in daily conversation, vary them, and use them so their "flavor" is brought out, you are capitalizing on this natural phenomenon of imitation.

Stimulating conversation which is neither "talking-down" to the child nor completely over his head will arouse the child's interest and curiosity about words and their meanings. At the same time the child will begin to grasp the meaning of various prefixes and suffixes which will increase his knowledge of words by leaps and bounds. To understand that *un-* means "not," can add *untie, untidy, undo, unwanted* and many others to the child's vocabulary, if the parent calls attention to these cues.

But why bother with all this? What is the importance of vocabulary for your child—and for you?

Vocabulary is related to many other skills such as understanding of reading matter and general intelligence. If you increase a child's vocabulary you also increase his ability to understand what he hears and what he reads. Besides being related to such academic skills it has long been noted that the vocabulary of successful business men is much larger than that of the average adult. But there is an even more important aspect which is perhaps so important that we take it for granted.

Words are our most important means of communication. We are all essentially alone in the world, for rarely can we make all our thoughts and feelings understandable to another individual. This feeling of isolation may be cherished by a few, but the majority of us like to share our thoughts with others. This becomes very difficult if we don't have adequate words at our command.

Words are not only our most important means of communication with others but they are our most important means of communication with ourselves as well. Try to think without using words—difficult, isn't it, if not impossible! A limited vocabulary, then, hampers your child's mental growth, his ability to think, and his most important means of communication with others. To develop these powers you can help your child in at least five different ways, none of them hard for either you or the child. Simply watch for opportunities to give him new experiences, "activate" the newly learned words, point out related words, use more stimulating conversation yourself, and show him how to analyze words as he comes across them in everyday life!

Sex Education

by KARL S. BERNHARDT

ONE of the greatest parental problems as well as the weakest part of child training today is sex education. Although many parents have advanced a long way from narrow Victorian secrecy about sex, this advance has still to be made by many others. They are very hazy as to how to approach the subject with their children. It should be said emphatically that it is the home that is primarily responsible for the job of sex and character education, and not the job of only the school, church and organized club. Sex education is bound up with the intimate, personal life of the individual and is not in the category of arithmetic and spelling.

For parents who find sex education embarrassing, self-education is in order. Reading, study and discussion help to develop an objective and impersonal attitude. A parent can practise hearing his own voice give a simple account of a child's growth in the mother's body, and the process of birth. He can also become familiar with and use technical terms that apply to parts of the body. Tone of voice and attitude are more important than the actual facts.

Children need information—not just facts, but more important, attitudes, the way facts are thought of, and the emotional coloring of them. The greatest danger is not ignorance, but wrong emphasis and misunderstanding.

Sex education goes on through childhood and cannot be a one-occasion, for-all-time lecture to an adolescent. Rather, it is a continuous process beginning in infancy. It is inevitable that children will receive a sex education, regardless of parents' role. Therefore a plan of education is essential.

When the child is ready for it, provide adequate information adapted to his understanding and which will satisfy his present needs. Develop in him a frank attitude toward sex, free from apprehension and worry. Build an attitude of acceptance of sex as an important but natural feature of life, with anticipation of participation in and enjoyment of the responsibility and joys of marriage and family life. Develop an understanding and acceptance of the necessary social conventions related to sex. Maintain confidence and trust so that he will always feel he has a source for honest information and a place to straighten out his fears and worries when they occur.

What to tell the child? The answer is plain—what the child wants to know. He is curious about everything —what makes the sun shine, where does the rain come from, why it gets dark, also where do babies come from, and why are boys and girls different. Natural curiosity should be satisfied, frankly and honestly. Of course a three-year-old cannot understand the complicated story of conception, development and birth, but he can understand how the baby is growing in mother's body, and how he is born into a wider world when he is strong enough. But this is only the beginning. During the school period there should be a continued discussion and expansion of understanding so that by the time the boy or girl reaches

114

puberty he will have fairly complete understanding as well as information. Parents' information may be supplemented by books, teachers and doctors—but the primary responsibility rests with the parents.

In the school-age period and adolescence sensible attitudes toward sex are of great importance. There should be family discussions about boy-girl relations, marriage and related questions. One important thing the growing child can receive from his parents is their help in developing a normal natural relationship with the opposite sex. Rigid restrictions of boy-girl relationships has been in some cases reasons for development of unwholesome relationships.

It is the responsibility of both parents to lay a proper foundation in early years for frank and open family discussions. Where the child experiences a silly or salacious attitude toward sex, he cannot help but build up the same attitudes. When he lives with people who have sensible, intelligent attitudes, his will becomes the same as theirs.

He needs more than just biological information—he needs to acquire a wider view of life, marriage and adulthood, of social conventions, of what is done and not done and why. He needs help all along the way to sort out the various ideas and attitudes he meets. It may also be desirable that the boy and girl know about some of the perversions of human sexual behavior. They cannot know the whole story of sex, but they should know that it can have unhealthy as well as healthy aspects. They should be told, for example, not to go off with strangers and be given clues as to the reasons why.

Our children today live in a world where sex is glamourized and degraded. They need knowledge and understanding to achieve a healthy, desirable attitude toward marriage, love and reproduction. We believe in the family as a unit of society, we believe in monogamy, and we believe in marital fidelity. We can help our children to believe in these as well. Above all, we need to have faith in our children.

Suggested Reading

Selected by TESS COGEN

FOR USE WITH CHILDREN UP TO AGE 12

GRUENBERG, SIDONIE, *The Wonderful Story of How You Were Born*, New York, Garden City Books, 1952, $2.50.

GRUENBERG, BENJAMIN C. and SIDONIE, *Wonderful Story of You*, New York, Garden City Books, 1960, $2.95.

LERRIGO, MARION O. and SOUTHARD, HELEN, *Story about You*, Washington, D.C., National Education Association, 1964, $.30. *Finding Yourself*, N.E.A., 1961, $.30.

FOR PARENTS

BARUCH, DOROTHY W., *New Ways in Sex Education*, New York, McGraw-Hill, 1959, $4.95.

Child Study Association of America, *What to Tell Your Children about Sex*, New York, Perma Books, 1964, $.50.

LERRIGO, MARION O. and SOUTHARD, HELEN, *Facts Aren't Enough*, N.E.A., 1962, $.30.

FOR LEADERS

Child Study Association, *Sex Education and the New Morality*, New York, Columbia Univ. Press, $1.95.

JOSSELYN, IRENE M., M.D., *The Adolescent and His World*, New York, Family Service Association, 1952, $1.75.

Siecus (Sex Information and Education Council of the United States) *Newsletter*, 1855 Broadway, New York, $2.00 annual subscription.

What Would You Do About
THE NEW BABY'S COMING?

By RALPH K. MEISTER

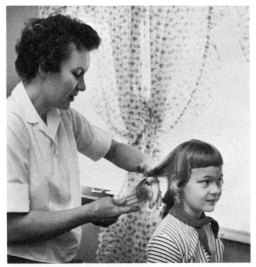

Ewing Galloway

The mother of five-year-old Janice is about two months pregnant and the question arises of when to tell Janice about the expected newcomer.

If you were Janice's parents, what would YOU do?

(a) Wait until mother returns trom the hospital with the new baby.

(b) Tell Janice right now that a new brother or sister is due in six to eight months.

(c) Wait until the fifth or six month of pregnancy when the new baby is "showing" to explain to Janice about its arrival.

(d) Tell Janice just before her mother has to go to the hospital, by way of preparing her for her mother's absence for a few days.

Discussion

It is considered good practice, to minimize jealousy of the new baby, to inform the older child some time before its actual arrival. Therefore, (a) and (d) would not be desirable since they would confront the child with a rather difficult adjustment just after or just before she was facing some deprivation of her mother's attention and affection due to her absence. On the other hand, (b) is not to be especially recommended since it subjects the child to the possibility of being confused or having to readjust should the mother miscarry and, in any case, imposes a considerable waiting time. (c) is probably the best procedure since it will give Janice time to gain some initial reassurance that she is still loved by her parents, is still important to them. It will also permit her to become accustomed to the idea of another baby by some participating and planning for its arrival. Whether or not Janice is told at this time about where the baby is, depends somewhat upon the parents' philosophy of sex education. Modern practice tends to a simple but factual presentation of these matters.

What Would You Do About
A MINOR ACCIDENT?

By RALPH K. MEISTER

Victor, age five, was playing a running game with a neighborhood dog in the course of which the dog tripped Victor who suffered some nasty scratches on his face and arms.

If you were Victor's parents, what would YOU do?

(a) Insist to the owner of the dog that he be kept on a leash.

(b) Forbid Victor to play with the dog again.

(c) Chastise Victor for being a cry-baby and for being clumsy.

(d) Personally punish the dog lightly with a switch to console Victor.

(e) Offer Victor your sympathy but point out that such accidents do happen.

Discussion

In rough-and-tumble play children do sometimes become painfully hurt. However, in general, the physical hurts are soon healed and sooner forgotten. To try to protect a child from these common accidents would almost amount to over-protection, to withdrawing him from normal interaction with his environment. Therefore (b) would not be desirable. Nor would (a) or (d) be recommended because they assume Victor has some legitimate complaint against the dog or his owner. This is not true and such an attitude on our part might encourage Victor to be looking for an opportunity to place the blame on somebody else whenever he ran into difficulty. On the other hand, alternative (c) is perhaps a little too harsh and unsympathetic. Alternative (e) seems most likely to give Victor the philosophical approach necessary to accepting such misfortunes in the proper perspective.

What Would You Do About
"TAKING CARE" OF BROTHER?

By RALPH K. MEISTER

Mother has asked Johnny, age five, to "take care of" his brother, Jimmy, age two, while she is busy in the kitchen. Johnny is taking his authority seriously and is surrounding Jimmy with so many "Don'ts" and "you-can't-have-its" that mother wonders whether he isn't using his position to take out some of the aggression he feels against his younger brother. Jimmy is objecting, not too quietly.

If you were Johnny's mother, what would YOU do?

(a) Ask Johnny what is the matter.

(b) Come in and re-define the situation so that Jimmy has a little more freedom of action under his fraternal overseer.

(c) Never give Johnny such an assignment because he will misuse it for his own ends.

(d) Scold Johnny for being mean and unkind to his brother.

(e) Bring both children into the kitchen under your watchful eye.

Discussion

We parents of more than one child are faced with the problem of finding socially approved channels for the expression of such a residue of jealousy as is left even after our best and sometimes heroic efforts to minimize it. This situation, where Johnny is given official blessing in a position of ascendency over his younger brother, seems to be one answer to this quest provided the domination is not overdone. Alternatives (a), (d), and (e) put Johnny on the spot and close this avenue of expression to him. (c) does the latter. He may have to take it out in teasing or other hostility to which we cannot turn a deaf ear or blink our eye. (b), used in a kindly, uncritical fashion, along with some note of appreciation to Johnny for his efforts in trying to help mother, should manage the situation very nicely. And it does have the dividend, by no means to be overlooked, of letting Johnny get out some of his hostility in a relatively approved manner.

What Would You Do About
A CHANGE OF HEART?

By RALPH K. MEISTER

Arthur, age five, has been justly reprimanded by his father for disobeying two previous injunctions not to stomp noisily through the living room and has gone to his own room sulking. Father is feeling a little sorry for Arthur and is tempted to go to him and make up.

If you were Arthur's father, what would YOU do?

(a) Curb the impulse since the reprimand was justifiable.

(b) Call Arthur in and tell him to stop his sulking since this in itself constitutes an offense.

(c) Have Mother go in and console Arthur.

(d) Wait until Arthur reappears and make some conciliatory remark.

(e) Try to engage Arthur in some play to distract him from his sulking mood.

Discussion

This problem illustrates the softheaded sentimentality in which we parents are all too often tempted to engage to the detriment of our disciplinary program and to the confusion of the child. When the child has been disobedient, it is our parental duty to reprimand him. Therefore alternative (a) is the best choice. None of the others can be recommended. (c) suggests a division of parental opinion which is not conducive to a consistent disciplinary regime. (b) is unduly repressive. The child cannot always take with equanimity the limits we impose. We should expect this and in general countenance it. Therefore, neither (d) nor (e) is recommended.

What Would You Do About

A PROMISE THAT CAN'T BE FULFILLED?

By RALPH K. MEISTER

Judy, age five - and - a - half, was promised a trip downtown by her mother, only to have an aunt whom she had never seen telephone to say she was in town on business and would like to drop in for a short visit.

Photograph by Harold M. Lambert

If you were Judy's parents, what would YOU do?

a. Tell Judy the trip is canceled because her aunt is coming to visit her.

b. Suggest meeting the aunt downdown and then returning home later with her, thereby giving Judy her trip.

c. Promise Judy two trips later.

d. Compensate Judy by a short trip to the ice cream store and possibly a small toy for the time being.

e. Tell the aunt you have promised Judy a trip downtown and so will not be home.

Discussion

This is a general type of problem which arises fairly often when we parents make a special promise to the child and may not be able to carry it out conveniently. (b) would be a happy compromise if it is possible under the circumstances. All too often, however, such a surprise visit necessitates doing certain things around the house before the guest arrives and (b) may not work. (e) is highly inadvisable if one wants to maintain cordial relations with one's relatives; the child is not the only one whose feelings must be considered. (a) expects too much philosophical resignation of a child that young. While the child must learn to take certain disappointments, we should avoid making them any more "crushing" than is absolutely necessary. (c) is rather meaningless to a child of this age for whom future pleasures are too dim to appreciably dull a present disappointment. Therefore, (d), though leaving much to be desired, is probably the best handling of the situation immediately. Arrangements should be made, however, for taking the trip later, preferably in the immediate future.

What Would You Do About THEFT?

By RALPH K. MEISTER

Richard, age six, steals things for which he has no use and which he doesn't want. He stole his father's pipe cleaners and hid them. His mother found the charred remains of her address book in the fireplace. He took the compact from the purse of a guest and dropped it out the window, apparently in order not to be discovered. He continues in spite of punishment.

What would YOU do?

a. Spank him very hard whenever he is caught and take away privileges.

b. Promise to give him what he wants when he asks for it so that he won't have to steal it.

c. Try to point out to him the antisocial nature of his actions and show him that people will not like him if he continues.

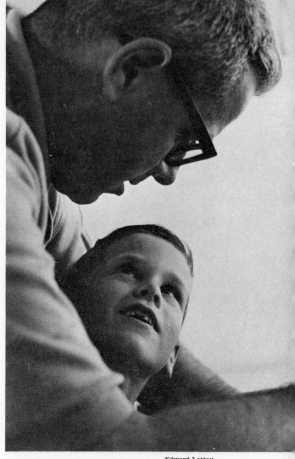

Edward Lettau

d. Give him more attention and cuddling and spend more time with him in storytelling and play.

e. Don't mention the matter to him at all but watch him so that he doesn't have a chance to steal.

Discussion

It is evident from the kind of stealing Richard does that he is doing it merely because he wants to get attention from his parents or wants to "get even" with them for not giving him as much affection as he needs. Therefore only "D" would get at the root of the problem. The others would be merely "treating the symptom." "A" would probably make matters worse because it would further deprive Richard of affection even though it might wipe out this particular symptom. "B" is irrelevant because Richard obviously is not stealing for possession. "C," used alone, is likely to prove as ineffectual as most pure lecturing. "E" would be impractical and would only postpone momentarily the time when the basic problem would have to be faced and handled.

What Would You Do About
THE NEIGHBOR'S CHILDREN?

By RALPH K. MEISTER

Carl, age six, a few afternoons each week usually brings home two or three playmates who proceed to play with such vigor, variety and originality that upon leaving no single toy is left untouched and the greater number are distributed over the floor. The task of restoring order is beyond Carl alone and you are getting a little tired of putting the mess in order, especially just before dinner time.

If you were Carl's mother, what would YOU do?

a. Wait until after dinner or before bedtime and then help Carl with the chore.

b. Meet the "delegation" at the door and suggest strongly that they play outdoors.

c. Tell Carl that he cannot have his friends in because they make too much of a mess.

d. Insist that Carl either clean up afterwards or be denied the privilege of having them over.

e. Cut down on the number of these visitations so that they will play at other homes as well as your own.

f. About ten minutes before the gang breaks up, have them all get together and set things in order.

Discussion

This is one of those administrative problems of parents which have psychological implications in that they affect the child's relationships with his playmates and with you as well. (b) and (c) are not fair to the children and (c) and (d) are somewhat unfair to Carl. (a), on the other hand, is not fair to you. (f) constitutes the best procedure in the long run. It does not arbitrarily penalize anybody but rather offers the children a workable solution. Oh yes, (e) is not a bad idea. Entirely apart from the issue of the clean-up, it is desirable for the children to meet at different homes.

What Would You Do About
FATHER'S ILL-TIMED TREATS?

By RALPH K. MEISTER

Evelyn, age six, and her brother, age four, rush up to greet their father upon his return home from work and he usually has some candy goodies for them. However, when they eat the candy this spoils their appetite for dinner.

If you were the parents of Evelyn and her brother, what would YOU do?

(a) Make them promise to save the candy until after dinner.

(b) Give the candy into Mother's safekeeping until after dinner.

(c) Take it away from them and give them none the next day if they begin on it before dinner.

(d) Let them have a little taste before dinner, saving the greater part until after the meal is over.

H. Armstrong Roberts

(e) Insist that they eat a certain amount of the dinner "no matter what."

(f) Have Father postpone giving them anything until after they have finished eating.

Discussion

This issue is a matter for parental unity. The most efficient and reasonable approach is (f). All of the others represent needless compromise which is difficult on all concerned. (a) would be an acceptable first step if it works, and it may. However, if it results in broken promises, such punishment as is involved in (c) is not good. (e) would probably create more problems and larger ones than the original. (d) would create a lot of fuss and even a "little taste" may take the edge off the children's appetite. (b) is not quite fair to Mother since it puts her in the position of withholding and, in addition, the sight of the candy may make the dinner less attractive. Father should be able to hold off with his largesse and, who knows, may he not in the long run be assured that they are running to greet him for himself and not for the goodies?

What Would You Do About
PUNISHMENT BY CONFISCATION?

By RALPH K. MEISTER

Robert, age six, received a gift of a much prized cowboy rifle, which popped paper with a gratifying, loud report. When he disobeyed his mother regarding crossing the street in front of his house, father was in favor of confiscating his gun, in other words punishing him by depriving him of the privilege of having the gun.

If you were Robert's parents, what would YOU do?

(a) Confiscate the gun but not permanently, just for a few days.

(b) Confiscate the gun and demolish it in the sight of Robert to indicate the permanent nature of his punishment.

(c) Let Robert keep his gun but tell him that since he obeyed so poorly you are not going to get him any similar gift the next time.

(d) Take the gun away and keep it until such time as Robert, by his good behavior, has earned the right to have it back.

(e) Leave the gun out of your considerations; punish Robert by depriving him of other privileges such as having him play indoors for the next day or two.

Discussion

The point of this quiz is to stress that a child's possessions should remain pretty much inviolate and their retention should not constitute a privilege. If Robert had misused the gun, say hitting another child with it, then taking it away might be justified. However, for disobedience, other fairer and more logical methods are at hand. Therefore, alternative (e) is the preferred one. Neither (a) nor (c) are particularly good. (b) and (d) are outstandingly bad, the first because it constitutes vindictive punishment and the second because it puts obedience and good behavior on a strictly "material reward" basis.

What Would You Do About
THE TOY-BREAKING CHILD?

By RALPH K. MEISTER

Tony, age six, seems to be playing in a rather destructive fashion with two of his trucks, greatly enjoying having them ram together and having one tip over the other. Father is concerned that the toys, though quite sturdy, may be damaged and even more important, he wonders whether such destructiveness is a good thing.

If you were Tony's parents, what would YOU do?

(a) Caution Tony to play more gently.

(b) Tell Tony that he may break one or the other of his toys and then he'll be sorry.

(c) Take the toys away from him for the time being so that he does not damage them and return them when he offers to play more constructively.

(d) Tell him that if he breaks either of the toys he should not expect you to replace or repair it.

(e) Chastise him for being so mean in his play.

(f) Just let him alone, allowing him to continue until he is tired of the activity.

Discussion

A child who is playing in this fashion probably has a lot of aggressive feeling to express, which dammed up might find expression in still less acceptable ways. Therefore, on the face of it, it might be best to use suggestion (f). Let him get it out of his system without your disapproving him. All the other alternatives, to a greater or lesser degree, attempt to suppress this expression of his emotion which is actually (barring the wear and tear on the toys) one of the least objectionable ways of his resolving his feelings. The toy truck that is getting the worst of the ramming battle may well represent a younger or older sibling against whom Tony is feeling a grudge. Or he may be acting out a protest against some slight he has felt from the person who gave him one of the trucks, a parent or relative or friend. In any event this kind of aggressive play, far from being a bad thing, may actually be a good thing from the standpoint of Tony's mental health.

What Would You Do About
NIGHTTIME FEARS?

By RALPH K. MEISTER

Kenneth, age 6, cries and refuses to go to sleep complaining that there are vague noises in the room that frighten him. He has a "sleeping light" on throughout the night but this is not reassuring in this instance. It appears to both parents that his fear is real rather than a simple stall to postpone bedtime.

If you were Kenneth's parents what would YOU do?

(a) Threaten to deprive him of the light unless he goes to sleep.

(b) Point out to him that there are invariably a lot of odd noises in a house but that no harm can come to him in his own home.

(c) Offer to trace down the noises to show that they are identifiable and of no importance.

(d) Tell him a six-year-old boy should be ashamed of being such a sissy, being afraid in a lighted room.

(e) Tell him how afraid you were as a child to point up how groundless are his fears.

(f) Lie down with him for a brief period and engage him in some other topic of conversation in order to calm him down and quiet his fears.

Discussion

The problem of how to soothe children when they are fearful is a common one. Alternative (a) would increase the child's fear, possibly even terrorize him. Neither (d) nor (e) are likely to provide him any special reassurance. (c) is ordinarily not feasible but may be attempted if there seems to be some definite identifiable noise. The alternative that should most definitely be used is (f). Our physical presence alone will do much to dispel the fear and relax the child sufficiently to permit him to drop off to sleep. The next morning we might supplement this with alternative (b).

What Would You Do About
DISCIPLINING PLAYMATES?

By RALPH K. MEISTER

ARTHUR, age six, has brought home a little school friend who is a bit on the boisterous and uninhibited side. After some preliminary rough-housing Arthur's friend is vigorously jumping up and down on the sofa when Mother enters. She is in no doubt about how she feels but, at the same time, she does sense that Arthur's friend is not her own son and that there is some question of how to proceed. *What would you do?*

(a) Call up the boy's mother and explain your complaint to her so that she may take appropriate action for her own son.

(b) Say nothing but glare eloquently in disapproval.

(c) Invite Arthur's friend to leave since he is not showing a proper respect for the home of his host.

(d) Tell Arthur and his friend that jumping on the sofa is forbidden and add at this time such rules for their play as seem necessary.

(e) Call Arthur aside and have him explain to his friend that his present actions are not increasing his popularity with you.

(f) Put up with this situation on this occasion but forbid Arthur to bring this boy to visit again.

Discussion

The purpose of this quiz is to point up the legitimacy of invoking "house rules" in situations involving children other than our own. In order that visitors to our homes should feel welcome and be welcome, we are justified in asking that they abide by our rules; or, "when in Rome, do as the Romans do." Therefore, (d) seems the best choice. (b), (c), and (f) do not give Arthur's friend a chance to know your complaint and to improve his behavior. (e) likewise introduces an intermediary when direct face-to-face action is more desirable. (a) seems undesirable not only because the boy's mother may take some offense at receiving a complaint regarding her son's behavior but because a solution of this issue from a distance (i.e., by the boy's mother) is not so practical as an "on-the-spot" handling of the situation by you.

What Would You Do About THE CHILD WHO CAN'T GET A WORD IN EDGEWISE?

By RALPH K. MEISTER

ROBERT, AGE SIX, has been trying to get into the dinnertime conversation but in the give-and-take between adults, he doesn't get in. He finally interrupts Father.

What would you do?

(A) LECTURE ROBERT on the impoliteness of interrupting adults.

(B) LET ROBERT APOLOGIZE and drop the matter.

(C) LET ROBERT CONTINUE with his interruption by deferring to him.

(D) FINISH YOUR OWN CONVERSATION very shortly and then give Robert an opportunity to talk.

(E) IGNORE HIS INTERRUPTION and talk above him so that he will find interrupting futile.

Discussion

Underlying any training in good manners must be a demonstration of the usefulness of such good manners. The child, in advertising terminology, must be "sold" on them. If they aren't useful and don't work for him, naturally he will not easily take to them. From this point of view, Alternative (D) seems the best procedure. (C) might encourage interruption. (A) and (B) are critical of the child without recognizing that he has a problem, and that there is no acceptable way provided for meeting it. Ordinarily we adults should pause every so often to give children a chance to contribute. We don't need to go to the extreme where the children do all the talking and we have to do the interrupting if we are to be heard. Alternative (E) would make for some mighty loud and even boisterous dinner conversation. don't you think?

What Would You Do About
THE CHILD'S BID FOR SYMPATHY?

By RALPH K. MEISTER

Edward Lettau

Lynn occasionally complains of a pain in her leg upon going to bed. The occasion occurs shortly after bedtime and seems to be a delaying tactic to get parental company and attention.

If you were Lynn's mother, what would YOU do?

(a) Be very firm and insist that Lynn go to sleep and forget the "pain."

(b) Point out to her that you think she is faking.

(c) Massage the leg sympathetically, tuck her in, and leave.

(d) Refuse to let her run around very much the next day to avoid the muscular over-exertion that may be causing such a pain.

(e) Give her an aspirin.

Discussion

Sometimes out of boredom a child may come up with such a complaint. To use methods (a) or (b) may make the child even more insistent on her affliction and it is always possible, of course, that there may actually be some slight discomfort present which the child is exaggerating and capitalizing upon. (c) seems the best approach since it does not give the child an opportunity to use the complaint to make an issue and fuss over it. (d) would give the entire matter undue importance, fix it in the child's mind and in that sense encourage hypochondriac tendencies. (e) is out unless you feel reasonably sure there is some very real basis for the complaint. For the psychological effect, you may want to use a sugar-pill if the wailing is unusually insistent.

In general, when children resort to such devices and it is not too unusual, we want to be understanding and sympathetic but we do not want to be dupes. Therefore, a token concession to the complaint with emphasis upon quieting the child for sleep is the best technique here.

Don't Hurt Me, Doctor

By GEORGE R. BACH

In dealing with emotionally disturbed children I see, on occasion, children suffering from rather strong fear of doctors and dentists. In some cases this is due to the unfortunate way in which the child was handled by a busy doctor who was seriously concerned with his physical ailment. Most doctors today are aware that the feeling of the child for him and his treatment have to be considered in working with him. Thus, in the majority of cases children's intensive fears concerning doctors and dentists, fears that handicap their adjustment to the usual routines of health procedures in schools, sports, etc., are not due to the faulty technique of the attending physician. You will find that today's physicians who work with children try to take a psychological approach to the ill child.

If this is true, you may ask why some children, and they may be yours, are afraid of doctors and dentists. Such fears, if not given psychological attention, may persist throughout the lifetime of the individual with the consequence that he may avoid medical care when it is actually needed, or may turn to open or disguised quackery.

Underlying these excessive fears in the child is what the psychologist calls "incompleted mastery" of conflict. Such children are tested with specifically designed psychological equipment which includes puppets representing doctors, dentists and nurses and a little stage-set-like dollhouse representing a doctor's office or a hospital. We encourage the child to work over his "medical experience" utilizing his rich fantasy by making up stories around that theme. Thus, for example, Johnny, age six, a husky, usually fearless boy who was referred for psychological study because of his excessive fear of doctors and dentists made up the following story as he manipulated the dolls:

Johnny placed the little boy doll, representing himself, on the operating table in the hospital stage set. The doll cries and pleads, "Please, Doctor, don't hurt me," but in spite of the boy doll's entreaties he is forcibly held down by the doctor doll who tells him to be quiet and do as he is told. Two nurse dolls then strap his arms and legs to the operating room table. Johnny then has the boy doll say to the doctor doll, "I don't like you; you are a big bad lion." The boy doll pulls his arm loose from one of the straps and hits the doctor doll, knocking him unconscious. A quick change of character role occurred at this point and Johnny had the little boy doll become the doctor and give first-aid to the unconscious doctor doll. The boy doctor is very gentle and sweet to the doctor-patient, tells him a story and brings him an ice cream cone. Again the role is quickly reversed and the boy doll is again the patient, but this time the doctor doll is very considerate of the boy doll patient. He does not strap him down to the operating room table, but holds him in his lap and tells him a story. The boy doll falls asleep on the doctor doll's lap and when he awakens the good doctor has made him well.

This is just one of the dozens of scenes and variations that Johnny made up about his medical experiences. While he was telling this story he looked up and said, "This is all make-believe, but some of it is true." This boy illustrates how important it is for a child to have an opportunity to relive through fantasy some of the fear experiences that he may otherwise forever associate with certain persons, in this case with doctors.

What you as a parent can do to prevent the fixation of these fears is to permit the child free expression about his medical experiences, let him have as much contact as possible with doctors, doctors' offices and hospitals under non-painful and non-anxiety-evoking circumstances. Above all, enter into his "playing doctor and nurse." Encourage him to go over his actual experiences or anticipated fears of the doctor's office, with his play equipment, using you, his mommy or daddy, as a prop. In this you will have to be prepared to play a role which might seem to you completely at odds with the real situation, such as the role of a "mean doctor" when you know, in fact, that the doctor is not mean at all. You will, undoubtedly, point out to the child that the real doctor wasn't mean, but what I ask you to do is to enter into the play in such a way that the child who had a fear or a momentary impression that the doctor could be mean has a chance to work out that fear and find a less frightening solution to the whole situation.

You may say that doctors, dentists, hospitalization, etc., are usually painful experiences for the child, that fear concerning them is only "natural" and has to be expected on the basis of physical pain. It is quite true that there is usually some physical pain connected with these experiences, but it is also true that, in many situations, such as playing in a gang, children get hurt much worse than in the doctor's office and think nothing of it. Consequently, it is how the child *adjusts* to the physical pain that makes the big difference.

I have here only discussed *some* of the ways in which you can help your child to overcome or prevent the occurrence of excessive fear of doctors. You will understand, of course, that any specific case of excessive fears may be severe enough to warrant professional psychological attention.

Character is like the foundation to a house—it is below the surface.

—WINDOW SEAT

Living With the Sick-Abed Child

By ELIZABETH M. FULLER

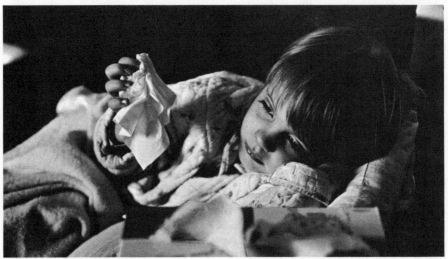

Edward Lettau

MOST MOTHERS would rather be mildly ill themselves than to have their preschool children mildly ill. Before we jump to the conclusion that mothers are too unselfish beyond the call of duty, or too lazy to care for their ailing families, let us look further into the problem of the sick-abed child. When a little boy or girl really is ill, the type of care required is usually clear cut and carefully prescribed by a physician. But when a mild illness keeps a child in bed for a short time or when a child is convalescing from a more serious illness, mothers must meet one of the most challenging problems of parenthood —how to keep the child relaxed and relatively content to stay in bed.

Mild illness and convalescence in children have characteristics in common. While their interests remain the same, there is an underlying irritability with inaction, a somewhat shorter than normal attention span, lowered energy and excitement needs, an exaggerated demand for adult attention, and a need for quiet yet engrossing entertainment.

The usual reading, coloring, music, radio, and TV routines might be thought of as filling in the gaps between other specially planned activities, but should not be considered as the *only* ways to fill up "sick" days. A little advance planning given to these inevitable "bad times" is extremely welcome when illness occurs and usually results in reducing the child's demands for adult attention at a time when the parent is busier than usual.

Let us assume, first, that some sort of worktable surface will be needed. A simple but entirely satisfactory bed table can be made by turning a lightweight cardboard carton upside down and rounding out the front, and back sides to make it fit easily over the child's legs.

An ordinary shoe bag with separate compartments may be safety pinned securely to the mattress at the side of the bed to hold small toys such as fig-

132

urines, crayons, postcards, small puzzles, or a favorite book.

For interest when "just reading," goldfish swimming in a bowl, a bird in a cage, a small turtle in a box, or a bird-feeding station outside the window gives a live touch to a sickroom. Also, a bean sprouting on a piece of wet cotton seems to grow before the child's very eyes in a few days' time.

For general interest, an old bedsheet taped to the wall with masking tape makes a delightful bulletin board for the child's drawings or for a funny picture Daddy made, or even for pictures cut out of magazines. Some parents have found toy balloons wonderful sickroom toys, one to blow and one or two colored balloons inflated and tied to the head of the bed with a three- to six-foot string.

A real treasure for the sickroom is a "surprise box" or "gadget box." Any old discarded box will do, but the main points to be considered are careful selection of "gadgets" to put into it, and seeing that it is kept away from the children until special need arises (such as illness, extended inclement weather, or a long automobile trip). The surprise or "new" element is important. Assembling its contents is a job which can be kept in mind along with ordinary housekeeping activities. There are no rules to follow except those related to safety (nothing sharp or lead-painted). Suggestions include paper clips, rubber bands, string, paper punch, padlock and key, small strainer, measuring spoons, pasteboard rollers from paper towels, metal hair curlers, coin purse with snap or zipper, chore ball, artificial flowers, rubber canning rings, clothes pins, old jewelry, buttons, shoe laces, or pieces of aluminum foil.

The list is endless, and the possibilities of independent sick-abed play unlimited.

When evening comes and fatigue and "let-down" feelings start to take over, simple shadow pictures on the wall are amusing. Mother and Daddy and the sick child can make them by placing a lamp in the proper position and manipulating the hands to cast shadows 'that look like heads of animals or various grotesque shapes. For variation, crumple a newspaper and arrange it in different positions on a table between the light and the wall to make many interesting shadow pictures.

All of these suggestions might be called "no-mess" activities. They are simple and they provide the sort of entertainment that is compatible with the sickroom.

There are many books available in retail stores which add to the list of things which can be done—if some judgment is exercised in selection. As a general rule, it is better to keep sickroom activities simple, to do one thing at a time, and if possible, to maintain a quiet and calm atmosphere. The mother who dashes in and out of the sickroom with quick staccato movements and a tense, high-pitched voice might well make a serious effort to "simmer down" and to realize she is setting the tempo for the child.

There is, of course, the possibility of overdoing efforts to make the sick room interesting, as Mrs. Dale will testify. Her Christopher, a very enterprising four-year-old, was caught in mid-December with his already sniffley head out of the window—"getting snowed-on so my cold will stay until we can finish my scrapbook. Gee, Mom, this is fun the way you play with me when I'm sick."

134   COMING HOME FROM SCHOOL can be a joyous occasion for the child if Mother is prepared
to listen to a recital of the day's events.

Developing Work Habits

By DOUGLAS F. PARRY

MANY CHILDREN who have difficulty in school are "poor" workers. Their mothers will say, "But I can't get him to do anything. He just won't settle down. He doesn't like to do his school work so he just doesn't do it. He will work if I stand over him, but he won't do anything for himself. He is too interested in swimming and baseball to do his lessons."

Undoubtedly the wisdom of a Solomon is required to solve some cases, but our suggestions to parents have proved useful in helping a number of children.

Decide with the child upon a plan of work. We will read for twenty minutes, do our arithmetic for twenty minutes, have a ten-minute recess, clean our room, and then you may go swimming.

Make a record of this plan and post it as a reminder and as a record of work accomplished. Activities to be accomplished may be listed in a column and checked off day by day: Reading, 20 minutes; Arithmetic, 20 minutes; Clean room, etc.

A mark of quality can be included also: excellent, good, fair, poor represented by letters or points. Any undesirable forms of behavior may also receive an accounting as: needed reminding, cried, forgot to bring his books home, and so forth. In any great undertaking, the initial steps include a plan, standard of work, and a measure of results.

Set the child's rewards and punishments in terms of his behavior. Allowances, television viewing, trips to the park, or permission to go swimming should be earned in terms of the child's performances and denied if he does not perform. This is the simple way of Nature: Nature is demanding and our lives are full or empty in relation to our productivity.

Show the child how to work. "Have a clean desk. Take out your reading book. Read the story and answer the questions. If you come to a word you do not know, look it up in your dictionary. If you cannot answer a question, read the story again. Write what the teacher tells you to do in your notebook. Do what you can do, then come for help." Sometimes, the key to success is to "narrow the field," to work paragraph by paragraph, to do the vocabulary exercises first, to discover what is to be done before reading the story, and so on. There is great value in discovering a step-by-step procedure of work. Children need to be shown how to work and to think and to search for answers.

Be certain that the level of work is manageable for the child. Fractions are impossible for the child who is uncertain of his basic multiplication facts. Geography is unmanageable for the child who is severely retarded in reading. Reading is too difficult for the child who stumbles over five or more percent of the words. While we must be challenged, nevertheless we must also understand in order to do.

Provide materials which will help the child to become an independent worker. A dictionary will reveal the meaning of a strange word. The index in our arithmetic book will tell us where to find the rules for dividing fractions. A notebook with a sample problem will remind us how to find a square root. A picture sound chart will help us sound out words. An answer key will permit us to discover whether our answers are right or wrong.

Be nonpersonal in demanding and evaluating work. It is *time* to work. We can't stop now because the work isn't finished. If we cannot work today, then we will have to do that tomorrow. The answer keys showed that five problems were wrong. We will work those over again until we get them all right. We can't go swimming because the work is not completed.

Always be willing to try a new way with new materials. When a child has had difficulty in learning to read with particular types of reading material, a new approach, a different kind of book, a fresh start are not only hope-bearing but often educationally wise.

Always be aware of possible causes for poor work. A great many children who dislike reading or who cannot manage arithmetic and therefore rebel against it have visual difficulties, hearing difficulties, or health problems. Some children's eyes do not coordinate and tremendous effort is required just to keep at the visual task of seeing. Some children have gaps in their learning because they do not hear certain sounds although they hear others. Other children are demineralized because of glandular or nutritional malfunctions and are restless, inattentive, and forgetful. Some failure to work might be due to simple rebellion against parents who are inconsiderate, inconsistent and unloving.

Mirror the child's behavior. Rather than become continually disturbed by the child who fusses about getting to work with "I don't want to, I am not interested in that, or why should I do that," mimic his behavior when he expects something from you. "I wasn't interested in getting dinner tonight. That's what you said to me this morning. I am not interested in taking you swimming. Why should I go to the movies with you? I don't feel like it." As a mirror helps adults look more as they wish, so a behavioral mirror affects children. But make it clear that you are imitating him and not accepting your response as a desirable one.

Control a variety of rewards. In our educational clinics at Drake University, we have a wealth of materials: rock collections, finger paints, interesting books, trains, model airplanes and automobiles, record players, moving picture machines, recording machines, building blocks, and so forth. But these are controlled for use as motivating forces for some children. To the child who does not wish to read but wishes to play with the train, we have a sequence of activities: "You read your lesson and then you may play with the train for a while. After you do these problems you can listen to yourself over the recording machine."

Maintain a life balance. While everyone must work, there should be time for play also. Some activity should be adult centered and adult directed, but some should be child centered and child directed. While there must be self-control and occasional painful effort to accomplish what life demands of us, so must there be occasional impulse and abandon for flavor and zest in living.

Those who learn to work meet life more efficiently and happily.

Comics and Television —
Their Influence on Children

By PAUL WITTY

EACH YEAR, SINCE 1950, the writer has made a study in April and May of televiewing habits and preferences of large numbers of boys and girls, their parents, and their teachers.

In our studies we found that over 90 per cent of boys and girls between eight and twelve years of age regularly read comic books; fourth, fifth and sixth graders were the most avid readers. Many of these children read six to nine comic magazines weekly; they might read even more from time to time. Boys were found to read comics somewhat more frequently than girls, but, generally, both groups were attracted to them. The attraction increased in the early grades and continued with consistency throughout the middle grades. In the seventh and eighth grades, interest in the comics continued. Here children were attracted, to them somewhat less frequently although many favorites of the middle grades still were read. The average number read by high school students was much lower than for junior high pupils.

The complaints against TV are similar to those directed against comics. Television, some parents charge, has usurped the leisure of children and young people, leaving little time for more desirable activities. "TV is converting children into a race of spectators," they say. "It's making children aggressive and irritable." "Overstimulating TV programs are giving our children tired eyes and sleepless nights." On the other hand,

Edward Lettau

some parents state that family relations and companionship have been improved as a result of TV.

One of the persistent criticisms of television relates to its adverse effects on study habits and scholarship. In several investigations, it became clear that the *amount* of televiewing is not related closely to intelligence or to scholarship. For example, one study ascertained the relationship between intelligence and amount of televiewing; the IQ's of pupils in grades three to six were correlated with the number of hours devoted to TV. The size of co-efficients was insignificant in every grade. Although there was very little correlation between educational-test results and amount of televiewing, excessive viewing did seem to be associated with somewhat lower academic attainment. This became clearer when the amount of time devoted to TV by pupils in the upper fourth of the group (their educational attainment measured by standard tests) was compared with time spent in televiewing by pupils in the lower fourth. Average time devoted to TV by pupils in the lower fourth was 26 hours per week, while that of the upper fourth was 20 hours.

Although TV does not, to a great degree, appear to influence educational attainment adversely, teachers and parents report individual cases in which its effects are undesirable. On the other hand, there are children who have been stimulated to do better work in school because of interests engendered by television.

Both teachers and parents continue to report behavior and adjustment problems which are associated with television—problems centered around increased nervousness, fatigue, impoverishment of play, disinterest in school, and eyestrain.

A group of school teachers made investigations of the children in their classes who were spending extremely large amounts of time televiewing. Some of the children were problem cases but others were well-adjusted, successful students. In every case of maladjustment, factors such as poor home conditions, lack of interest, unfortunate experience seemed to contribute to the child's difficulties—TV alone could not be held responsible for the undesirable behavior. Some pupils who spent a very large amount of time with TV were good students while other such viewers were very poor in school work. These teachers concluded that a fair appraisal of the desirability or undesirability of televiewing could be determined only after making a complete case study of each child.

So, too, in the case of comics. It would be unjustifiable to attribute such a complex condition as a child's poor scholarship, or very undesirable conduct, solely to his reading of comic magazines. Well-adjusted pupils who are good students, like less well-adjusted pupils, often read great numbers of comics. Yet, for a particular child, the comic magazine might provide additional stimulus to undesirable behavior.

Good Books in the Home give the child an alternative to television. Too much TV viewing sometimes is simply the result of boredom.

Dirt and Douglas

By ELIZABETH MECHEM FULLER

The other day Mrs. Brown stopped by. She brought her troubles with her seven-year-old son, Douglas, into the office to seek help. After a fairly long chat, her troubles resolved themselves into one basic issue—namely, the pitched battle the American housewife (or house-husband) wages against dirt and disorder. This issue is so common that it deserves much more attention than it gets. Our American obsession for sterile cleanliness and orderliness caused a visiting student from a European country to remark recently, "My first impression of your country was amazement at how you scrub your lives away. On my first trip downtown in one of your large cities, the bus stopped at a station which was next door to a big super-market. This market had two enormous windows filled to overflowing with nothing but soap chips, soap flakes, soap liquids, soap bubbles, soap powder, soap bars, soap granules—yes, even soap ducks and soap rabbits. I went into the bus station and sat down to rest in the ladies' lounge. The radio was playing music offered by one soap company, and then the program changed to a drama offered by—sure enough — another soap company. Every woman and child that came into the ladies' lounge headed straight for a wash basin and scrubbed something. Gradually, I was more amused than amazed, because my later impressions, based upon longer acquaintance, didn't change very much. You do truly scrub your lives away."

While there may be some exagger-ation, in general, she is right. But even more serious, we sterilize our human relationships to the point of extermination—particularly where young children are concerned. There is something paradoxical about a society that preaches endlessly about social and emotional security and then sets such high standards of order and cleanliness in its homes that its children are literally forced right out of them to any place where there's some good constructive dirt and "goo," and some measure of freedom in manipulating the environment. All too familiar is the child from a too-clean and orderly home who prefers to rendezvous with the dirtiest child in the neighborhood and chooses his home for his regular visits. Mrs. Brown, for example, reported that Douglas "invariably sneaks off to play in the cow barns." She told of forbidding him to play on the floor in any home where they

Ewing Galloway

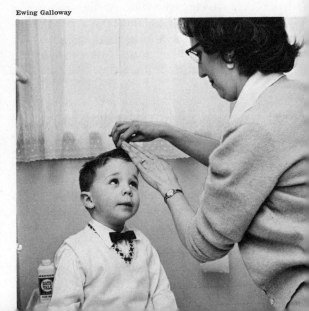

139

keep pets, of insisting that he even *sweep* his room after a play session, of following him around picking up after him, of his refusal to keep his hair combed. Mrs. Brown described a perfect example of producing sterility in human relations alongside germ-free and dirt-free body, clothing, and home.

As a nation which boasts of the most bathtubs, the best dissemination of health information, the "highest" standard of living, its citizens are bewildered at the staggering figures on *mental* health or the lack of it. Is it just possible that soap has been substituted for a real interest in children and their sound, balanced development? Are the bathtubs being used enough for water play (which includes splashing the floor)? Does our public health information tell also about the reduction of children's resistance to disease when they meet too few germs and too little dirt at an early age? Does the "highest" standard of living include a serious evaluation of the *feeling* side of its children and adults?

No one likes to live in a home where there is needless dirt and chaotic disorder. That is as demoralizing as the home with too-high standards. Nevertheless, there is a happy medium in which dirt and disorder might be endowed with personality, to illustrate the point. Then what is advocated is "constructive dirt" and "meaningful disorder." A home with "constructive dirt" and "meaningful disorder" takes on that lived-in look. The true test of a home of this sort is its visible evidence of the interests and hobbies of each of its members. In looking at many modern homes, a visitor cannot tell the ages of its residents, or cannot even tell how many persons live in it. In a lived-in home

which houses children, a visitor might see cut-out stickers reflecting the season pasted on the windows, a roughly laid out flower bed with botchy signs in a childish scrawl at the corner of the yard, a model airplane on the living room table, children's books on the end tables alongside adult literature, a pair of skates just outside the kitchen door on the porch, an awkwardly assembled bouquet of wild flowers on a table, a dish of gum drops alongside the adult treat, a torn doll dress in the mending basket—these are visible symptoms of the parental point of view that "our children live here too." Forgiven instantly, should be the parent who apologizes for the slight disorder in her house by saying, "I'm sorry, but the children and I just couldn't resist this beautiful sunshine for a walk in the woods." Usually, with careful planning the house can be put in order *and* the children taken for a walk in the woods, but when such opportunities arise spontaneously and a choice must be made — then an apology for the house seems in order at least once in a while.

Mrs. Brown's intentions were of the best; she unquestionably loved Douglas. As she talked she came to see how she had been making repeated decisions favoring her neat and well-ordered house at the expense of her boy's happiness and general adjustment. As a result, Mrs. Brown's Douglas has a surprise coming the next time he digs worms and goes fishing in the creek, because Mrs. Brown is going to offer to clean his "dirty old fish" and fry them in her spotless kitchen. That is her first step toward having a lived-in house with reasonably happy people living in it.

Parent-Child-Teacher Relationships

FROM THE VIEWPOINT OF THE SLOW READER

By ALFRED SCHMIEDING

We have long recognized that the parent-child relationship is an important factor in the educational growth and emotional development of the child. In recent years the teacher-child relationship has also come in for considerable study, since it was realized that this, too, will influence the child favorably or otherwise. Here, then, is a triangular situation — parent-child-teacher — that is normal and socially acceptable, unlike another triangle which comes to mind.

Broadly considered, this triangle opens up a large area of potentialities and implications. But for the present let us focus the attention on the interrelationships when the problem is complicated by a child's slowness in advancing in reading ability.

Parents soon notice when their child is not progressing in reading as he should, and so do teachers, of course. The parent may compare the child's progress with that of an older brother or sister, or with the child of a relative, friend, or neighbor. If the parent makes this comparison mentally and does not bring the observation into the open by word or action, there is less likelihood of adverse influences on the child. But where is there a parent who can remain calm and fully discreet in the face of such a difficulty?

If, then, the mother or the father or both feel and say, *"I have always said that the way teachers teach reading nowadays is all wrong; it's positively stupid!"*, the child may feel he is being protected from unfair circumstances. Thus, the child's relationship toward his present teacher may become one of hostility or lack of confidence in her. He will then act accordingly, and his reading difficulty will remain shelved for the time being as a consequence.

If, in addition, the parents give vent to their opinion about modern teaching methods to relatives or friends in the presence of the child, he will be careful to note their reactions. Possibly he may feel he is getting a "raw deal," that he is being "gypped." Again, his reading difficulty remains on the shelf, only it is pushed back a little farther.

Perhaps the parent will decide to pay a visit to the school. This is, of course, proper and correct. Parents and teachers need to consult for the child's sake. If only the parent pro-

141

ceeds from a forthright basis of finding out what the difficulty is or how the situation can be helped, much may be gained. But if the parent sallies forth with a chip on the shoulder or with the idea of putting her ideas about reading into practice, the visit is likely to have an adverse effect on the child. If the parent visits the school regularly to check up, the child will soon get the feeling, "My mother is fighting my battles for me; I should not worry." And so there has developed another over-protected child. This has happened despite the fact that the parents were sincere and aware of their responsibility.

The teacher, as the third member of the triangle, is in a difficult situation. She may have already consulted the adjustment teacher or the reading specialist. The child's reaction to this may be that other persons are taking up his case. His feeling of being protected has not been weakened. Some one will find a solution for his problem. That suits him fine.

By this time the teacher as well as those whose advice she has sought may conclude, *"This is not a reading problem mainly. It may have been that as a start, but it has now become a problem of emotional adjustment."* The more the teacher does for the child, the harder she tries, the less the child does for himself—in fact, his efforts to learn to read are at a low minimum.

The teacher is, of course, on the defensive toward the child, but even more so toward the parent. Being human, she must talk to someone. She pours out her heart to other teachers and in doing so uses some choice and neatly descriptive expressions. It *could* happen that the child might overhear these discussions!

But even if he does not overhear the conversations, he nevertheless senses the crackle in the emotional climate. Thus he has been trapped in an interpersonal relationship — a triangle — which leaves him utterly confused.

Since it was not the intention to write a tragedy and leave the matter there, a sequel is called for in the form of a happy ending.

Mother and Teacher meet again at a later time on a more friendly and cooperative basis. Both express their regrets of the things that have been said and done. The adjustment teacher is called in for advice. Teacher and Mother agree on a plan for Son or Daughter. Son or Daughter notices and wonders. Father is part of the plan. He plays his role well because he "sees sense" in the approach. The general idea underlying the plan is that the child will be called on to work fairly independently on reading material that is interesting and new to him and on a level which makes reading relatively easy for him. The program combines reading, filling in blanks, making sketches, re-arranging words, and similar activities.

Some time later the child even feels the thrill of doing a job with little help from anyone. One evening, still later, he shows his work to Father and says, *"Look, Dad!"*

JUST BOY

A boy if not washed too often and kept in a cool, quiet place after each accident, will survive broken bones, hornets, measles, fights and nine helpings of pie.

A boy is a piece of skin stretched over an appetite; a noise covered with smudges. A boy is the problem of our times, the hope of the world. Every boy born is evidence that God is not yet discouraged with men.

Guidance in Human Relations in School

By RUTH STRANG

Every classroom and playground is a laboratory in which children learn human relations. Group experiences with other children, beginning with the small home and neighborhood groups, are indispensable for social development.

During their preschool years children are already learning to relate themselves to others of their own age. This is good preparation for entering kindergarten and first grade. The process of learning about human relations gives rise to sympathetic behavior, along with some transitory quarreling and hitting.

Some of the best guidance is done by the children themselves. When Teddy, an outgoing, well-adjusted little boy, did an excessive amount of hitting and teasing, the other children said, "Teddy, you're a naughty boy. You can't play with us until you stop hitting." Sometimes, however, children do not act so wisely. Two children were playing together when a third child came along and wanted to join them. They chased him away, although he came back several times saying, "Let's be friends."

Parents can make their child's friends welcome. One boy realized this when he said, "My Daddy wouldn't chase any of my friends the way some other daddies do." This child's parents had made a real effort to attract other children to him. For summer days they made a wading pool in the backyard, which any of his friends might use. On hot afternoons the children came, wearing their bathing suits, ready to enjoy the

fun. Teachers often seek parents' help in widening a child's circle of friends.

In a day-care program for school-age children, the teacher of the group of five- to six-year-olds was particularly sensitive to the development of their social behavior. Sidney, one of the smallest children in the group, was extremely noisy and aggressive; he took every possible means of making himself seen and heard. He resented any show of affection by the teacher on the ground that "he was not a baby." Gladys talked continuously in a loud high-pitched voice. She was unhappy if another child was chosen instead. She would sometimes sit in the teacher's lap and say, "I'm your baby." The teacher's guidance of these two children consisted largely of being so kind and thoughtful of them that they felt less need to use socially unacceptable ways to win love and recognition.

The New York Times

143

Maria, another girl in the same group, had not spoken a single word to anyone since she joined the group in the fall. At first the other children would have nothing to do with her, because she wouldn't talk to them and because, as they said, "She stinks." The teacher asked the public health nurse about Maria's home conditions, and especially about the facilities for bathing and washing clothes. The nurse enlisted the help of an older sister, a Girl Scout, in sending Maria to school clean and neat. The teacher herself was friendly to Maria without singling her out for special attention. By the end of the year she was fully accepted by the others and had learned to enjoy playing with both small and larger groups.

The most aggressive boy in this group was Carl. He could not accept authority or reproof. If anyone hit him first, he would not be satisfied until he had really hurt the other child. When anything aroused his anger, he would kick and hit and swear at the other children, threatening to kill them with his father's gun or have his older brother beat them up. After exhausting himself in one of these outbursts, he would withdraw from the group a while, and later try to win back their acceptance. Whenever the teacher gave him recognition and the children invited him to join in their play, his face lighted up with a winning smile.

Though Carl was one of the youngest children in the group, he was also the biggest. He was proud of his superior strength. He liked to defend others and was hardly ever daunted by the size of his adversaries. One day the teacher found Carl planning to fight with a larger boy whom he was quite sure he could beat. The teacher promised at some later time to give each boy a pair of boxing gloves so that they could see which was the better fighter. Carl seemed quite satisfied with this suggestion.

Carl was very slow in relating himself to the teachers and resisted their attempts at friendliness. He had to feel quite sure of an adult before he would trust him.

In this complex and difficult case, the teacher recognized the child's deep-seated hostility, his distorted home relationships, his lack of affection from the persons who meant most in his life. She also realized that his uncontrollable outbursts of anger probably frightened him and increased his underlying insecurity. She tried to understand the meaning which his behavior had for him. In this informal group she was able to modify his environment enough so that he could usually handle it successfully. This gave him confidence and a feeling of success. In cases like this the child's social relations in school reflect his personal problems and home relationships.

CHILDREN

Two educators who have made a three-year study of child rearing have counted 18,121 assorted satisfactions, as contrasted with only 7,654 headaches to be found in the rearing of children.

—QUOTE

What it Means to be a Slow Reader

By JOSEPHINE A. PIEKARZ

WHO ARE THE CHILDREN who become the slow readers? In most respects they are no different from those who learn to read well. They come from all nationalities and socioeconomic classes. For reasons yet undetermined slow readers are most often boys. In most instances they are average or bright children. They come from small classrooms as well as overcrowded ones. They are often successful in such subjects as arithmetic, science, and geography, but have difficulty learning to read.

Realizing how important reading is in all phases of our society, all parents hope that their children will learn to read well. For the child who does not learn to read has a difficult time meeting many of his everyday problems. The longer he continues to remain a slow reader, the greater his problems become.

Many people are involved in the child's failure. First, the child himself is disturbed. He does not wish to be a reading failure. It is doubtful whether there is any child who does not want to learn to read. He may say so when he has experienced failure for a period of time, but it isn't really true. The most frustrating part of his failure is that it isn't entirely his fault. Yet he is unable to do anything to help himself. No wonder he has a deep sense of hopelessness.

Second, the child's whole family is intimately involved in his problem. He may be considered a disgrace to the family. He may be the only one in the family who isn't a good student. He may be compared unfavorably to his brothers and sisters. His parents' attitudes toward him may be influenced by his inability to read. The parents may feel guilty or responsible in some way for his failure. Often strong feelings develop between parents and child over the reading failure. These attitudes are frequently carried over into all other phases of the child's home life. Reading failure cannot be overlooked so long as the child is in school.

Third, the child's classroom teacher is also deeply concerned with the child's problem. She is acutely aware of the severity of his difficulties. She may even feel partly responsible for his lack of progress. She may try to make his problem as inconspicuous

Ewing Galloway

as possible by assigning him only work he can do, by calling on him to recite only when she is sure he can do so, by praising him lavishly when he does something well, and by emphasizing his strong points. She may want to give him extra help but this may be impractical, if not impossible, in a classroom filled to capacity or even overcrowded.

Despite everything a teacher does, she cannot keep from the child the knowledge that he is not reading as well as other children in his room. He realizes this whenever he hears the other children read. They also are aware of this and can make his life miserable by thoughtless teasing. This places an added responsibility upon the teacher. If she is sensitive to the situation, school may become a nightmare for her as well as for the child.

How does the child adjust to his lack of progress while all those around him are learning to read? Individual children react in different ways, depending upon their basic personality pattern and the attitudes of the people around them. Some show little concern—outwardly. They avoid reading activities as much as they can and seem to derive satisfaction from the things they are able to do well.

Others, thoroughly convinced they are stupid, develop feelings of inferiority and insecurity and tend to withdraw into themselves. They grow to fear books, teachers and school. They may resist going to school; they may make a scene or may actually become ill each morning when it is time to start out. In school they cause no disturbance for they just sit quietly and daydream. Very often the class-work may be beyond their level and they may derive very little from school attendance.

Still others become behavior prob-

lems. Because they do not succeed in reading, they seek the attention they need in other ways. They become aggressive and noisy. They declare loudly that they hate reading, that it bores and tires them, that it is a waste of time, that they would rather spend their time on interesting things. And often, it is true. They are bored with the childish books they are given to read. They do many things to distract the teacher's attention. They get into mischief in school, on the playground and at home. They seem to be out of step with society. They go around with an attitude challenging others to belittle them. This will give them an excuse to fight back and maintain their self-esteem.

Regardless of the child's adjust-everything possible to help the slow-reading child. Frequently, however, cannot read, he is a child apart from other children.

Parents are usually anxious to do everything possible to help the retarded reader. Frequently, however, they do not know what to do or where to go. Sometimes they transfer the child from one school to another; in their overzealous efforts to co-operate with the school, they often create misunderstandings. Still others attempt to teach the child themselves with little or no success.

Many modern school systems employ reading specialists who work in close co-operation with the classroom teachers. Perhaps the reading specialist should be called upon personally to help the child overcome his difficulties; or individual instruction in a reading clinic for a period of time may be the best solution.

In any case, it is important to identify the slow readers early and help them overcome their difficulties in order to avoid the unhappiness that will otherwise follow.

The Gifted Child Sometimes Has Reading Problems

By RUTH STRANG

SOME GIFTED CHILDREN read too little; they have not developed their reading potentialities. A few read too much; they use reading as an escape from their other developmental tasks. Let's try to find out why.

Why are some children and young people poor readers when they could be superior readers? Why do they sometimes fail in school when they could be able learners? There are many possible reasons.

They may have become disillusioned with reading in early school years. Those who learned to read before going to school may be bored by inane primers. We can sympathize with the disappointment of the six-year-old who had expected to read about the new and fascinating world which had been revealed to him in earlier books; when he found the printed words merely said, "The boy can run," he said, "I didn't need to learn to read to know that." As they continue through school, gifted children may find the reading material they are offered dull and unrelated to their lives; it does not seem worth efforts to read. Unless parents and teachers identify the potentially able children and provide suitable reading experiences for them, these youngsters may become indifferent to reading and dissatisfied with school.

To prevent the occurrence of this state of affairs, one school formed small groups of fifth- and sixth-grade

Edward Lettau

superior readers. The groups met for one forty-minute period each week. One week they spent the period in the library where the librarian introduced them to biography, stories from foreign lands, and other kinds of literature. The next week they came together for a period to discuss books they had read. The children spoke with enthusiasm about this experience. Parents might suggest similar means for enriching the environment of gifted children in their local schools, or provide it in their homes.

Attitudes toward gifted children also may prevent the youngsters from using their talents. Adolescents do not want to stand out from the crowd. They resent teachers who, by calling attention to their special abilities, may alienate them from their classmates. Gifted youngsters often say, "The other kids don't like me." So they try to be like the other kids by concealing their interest in serious reading and scholarship. As one teen-age girl said, "If you're taller than boys, that's bad enough, but if you're brighter, it's fatal."

Failure to concentrate on reading and study also may be traced to home worries. The child is preoccupied with emotional conflicts growing out of family relations—the quarreling of parents who disagree, or seem on the verge of getting a divorce; the jealousy of brothers and sisters. One child could not keep his mind on school work because he kept thinking of his younger brother at home with his mother, doing interesting things with her, shutting him out from the close relationship he so much desired. When the mother understood how the boy felt, she made it her business to give him time every day that was exclusively his.

Sometimes failure to read is an expression of hostility toward a parent. Perhaps the child feels his parent does not really care for *him* but only for his achievement—only that he be "a credit to the family." If the situation looks this way to the child, the parent should make an effort, in many casual ways, to show the child real affection. This cannot be done by merely saying "I love you" or by giving the child presents. Affection may even be expressed by punishment that the child recognizes as necessary for his best development.

During later adolescence a conflict regarding vocational choice may deflect a youngster's attention and effort from his school work. In one case, the father wanted his son to follow in his footsteps and become a doctor. The boy had no interest in this profession and little aptitude for it; he wanted to go into business. He flunked out in the freshman year of college. He was referred to a reading clinic where his problem was recognized as lack of desire rather than lack of ability to succeed in college. After skillful counseling had resolved some of the conflicts, he was able to put his mind on his college work and go ahead successfully toward the vocation of his own choice.

Many young people are achieving far below their capacity because they lack a sense of purpose and social responsibility for their gifts. "So what?" is their attitude toward their mediocre performance. For these youngsters biographies and stories of people who have caught and "followed the gleam" are inspiring. They identify themselves with persons who have made good and have contributed to human welfare.

And what about the gifted children who use reading as an escape from realities and responsibilities? It sometimes happens this way: The child finds it difficult to make friends because he has not played much with other children. To alleviate the pain of social failure, he turns to reading. Here he is successful. But he is not getting the social experience he needs. Consequently, he finds increasing difficulty in relating himself to others. His scores on reading and intelligence tests are very high. Teachers and parents may encourage his intense interest in books. Eventually, he may make an important specialized contribution to society, but it will be at the expense of his personal happiness. Probably he also will not realize his full capacity for social achievement.

These problems need not arise. If the total developmental needs of the gifted child are recognized and met, his reading can be a source of inexhaustible pleasure and his most important way of learning.

Leisure Time Activities for the School Age Child

by KARL S. BERNHARDT

No one today doubts the importance of leisure time activities in the lives of school children. Through these activities important features of character and personality, initiative, resourcefulness, and the fine art of enjoyment are developed. There is no lack today of entertainment, there is probably an over-emphasis of it. Many children spend endless hours with their ears glued to the radio, or their eyes to the television. These "passive" pursuits have an important place, but not if they crowd out more active leisure time activities.

SOME LEISURE TIME ACTIVITIES THAT CHILDREN ENJOY:

1. *GAMES.* Sports and athletic games are many and have become well known through their use in schools, camps, etc. It is important that they should not be too complicated for the child, and competition should not be over-stressed. There are also games for home—cards, checkers, parchesi, puzzles, and games of skill in which several people can take part. These provide an opportunity for learning both to win and lose gracefully.

2. *HANDICRAFTS, BUILDING and CONSTRUCTION.* Nothing is quite as satisfying as making things, and there is an almost unlimited variety of materials to use for projects —wood, leather, plastics, clay, paper, yarn, cloth, linoleum. A place to keep materials and tools, a place to use them, and some help and encouragement are all needed for creative activities.

3. *ARTISTIC and DRAMATIC ACTIVITIES.* A child should be free to experiment and create—to sketch, paint, model, or carve. Music can be an absorbing and enjoyable activity for leisure time provided it is not limited merely to adult-imposed music lessons. Records, family orchestras, concerts and radio are all aids to music appreciation. Dancing can be a happy form of expression and an aid to coordination and poise. Dramatics can be enjoyed through watching a play or participating in it. Marionettes and puppets can satisfy the school age child's desire to be an actor. Dressing up, using make-up or putting on a circus performance can become a happy occasion.

4. *EXPLORING* nature and the world around us is an endless source of joy and education. A child discovers that so many wonderful things happen out-of-doors, and he doesn't have to go to the zoo or the country to see things—wind, sunsets, frost, insects, and flowers. These can be found in his own yard. Then there is ASTRONOMY. This may interfere with bedtime occasionally, but the values and fun received from the study should be ample compensation. A small telescope, charts of the heavens, and simple astronomy books are all that are needed if the child has a parent or friend to share the interest with him. Pets and the care of them are a natural interest. There is an endless variety: kittens, dogs, canaries and parakeets, white rats or mice, guinea pigs, rabbits, fish and turtles. For the city child, trips to a farm to see the

domestic animals, and to get to know them can be fun and an education. The world of exploration includes nearby points of interest as well as more distant ones. Factories, stores, the railroad station and postoffice, are just a few places where children can see, learn and gain an appreciation of the kind of world in which they live.

5. *HOME ARTS. Cooking.* Both boys and girls have fun producing culinary masterpieces for the rest of the family to enjoy. Materials, opportunity, and a little guidance are necessary, together with a feeling of freedom. *Gardening.* There are many thrills in growing things. To be a truly leisure time activity it must be the child's own garden and he must be free to care for it because he wants to.

6. *COLLECTIONS.* Making a collection of anything—stamps, coins, matchbox folders—classifying, mounting, and caring for it gives pleasure and has value.

7. *READING* opens up great new worlds to the child, but it should not become too prominent and push aside more active forms of pleasure. The child needs some guidance but should not feel that the adult is selecting the books or imposing his own standards of what is worth reading. He may read "trash" (to adults) but the important thing is that he learn by so doing, to discriminate between "good" and "bad" literature.

PRINCIPLES OF PLANNING FOR LEISURE

Time. It is necessary to plan the child's day so that there is time for him to follow his own interests, time as uninterrupted as possible, time he feels is his own. The parent should not desire nor attempt to make every moment count.

Materials. Most leisure activities require materials of some kind—equipment and tools to use for creative projects. Provide these for the child's expressed interests. Start with the simplest equipment, gradually increase the amount and kind as interest continues and grows. Provide materials in terms of the child's age and ability.

Place. Children need a place to keep their materials, tools, and collections, as well as a place to use them. Shelves and cupboards are necessary and there should be requirements about putting materials away and clearing up.

Attitudes. Attitudes of the parents and other adults have a great deal to do with development of interest in the child. Interest breeds interest. Many activities which are valuable to the school age child do not seem worthwhile from an adult point of view. Adults should respect the child's choice of activity and give plenty of encouragement and help in terms of stimulating him to choose and initiate activities for himself.

A variety of interests is desirable; too much specialization is to be avoided, and the emphasis should be on the enjoyment of the activity more than the achievement.

The child's leisure should be spent both in and out of the family home. The family is a more effective unit when there are plenty of family excursions, games, music and art craft activities. But there should also be a recognition of the importance of the child's having interests beyond the family circle.

Nowadays life can be so strenuous and serious that play is even more important than usual. Let's help the child to play, and let us not forget to play, too.

What Would You Do About
THE CHILD WHO WANTS TO HELP?

By RALPH K. MEISTER

Sharon, age seven-and-a-half, comes into the kitchen where Mother is baking a cake and, obviously bored with play, wants to help. Sending her to the basement to help Father is out because he has just sent her up to help you.

If you were Sharon's mother, what would YOU do?

a. Suggest some game for her to play by herself.

b. Let her watch you in your activity, explaining to her what you are doing.

c. Let her busy herself in helping by handing you items or taking dishes to the sink.

d. Give her some ingredients to mix for herself.

e. Let her help with the mixing or with greasing the pans.

H. Armstrong Roberts

Discussion

At the risk of some difference of opinion because the best psychology may not necessarily be the best way to bake a cake, alternative (e) is recommended. Sharon is old enough to be competent in supervised participation and the success of the venture will not only give her a sense of achievement but be educational as well. For this same reason (d) is not recommended here though a flour and water mixture might be appropriate for a younger child. (c) is not recommended because it may be too dull and discourage the child's possible interest and eventual skill. (b) would almost certainly be dull. (a) is a method of getting rid of the child, maybe. However, parenthood should have more positive goals than simply avoiding nuisance.

What Would You Do About UNEQUAL COMPETITION?

By RALPH K. MEISTER

BILLY, age seven, has engaged Father in a little game of marbles. However, Father's superior skill, a holdover from his own boyhood days, is turning the scales strongly in his favor. As Billy is close to losing all his marbles, he is making up new rules, even cheating a little. He seems close to tears at the prospect of defeat.

What Would You Do?

(a) Point out to Billy that he is cheating and that this isn't good sportsmanship.

(b) Play the game strictly according to the rules and may the best man win.

(c) Refuse to play further with Billy because he is being a sissy and a poor sport.

(d) Continue playing but let up enough so Billy has a chance of at least breaking even and possibly besting Father.

(e) Show Billy you are intentionally letting him win.

(f) Don't play such games in the future.

Discussion

Perhaps the first observation to make in this discussion is that sportsmanship assumes first of all opponents who are fairly evenly matched. This is not the case here so considerations of sportsmanship seem a little out of place. Certainly one wouldn't seek to apply them if the competition were in wrestling where the unevenness of the match would be somewhat more evident. Neither (a), (b) nor (c) seems apropos for these reasons. (f) is rather an extreme solution and deprives both father and son of their close association. In general, in Billy's eyes Father is so wonderful and all-powerful that unless Billy can occasionally get some experience of successful competition with his father, he may feel worthless by comparison. This is certainly not an attitude we would wish to develop. Therefore, (d) would probably be the best choice here. Only as Billy builds his own self-confidence and skill can we expect him to play the game with sportsmanship. Otherwise he will simply seek to avoid the frustration of defeat by any means possible, poor sportsmanship and cheating among them. (e) would be a little unfair since it would be giving Billy a hollow victory and could only increase his frustration and even threaten him more since he would seem to be not even worthy competition for his dad. Oh yes, this is a kind of cat-and-mouse situation and as such does constitute actually teasing Billy if Father really played to win.

What Would You Do About
ACCIDENTS?

By RALPH K. MEISTER

Kathie has just spilled her milk all over the table, but has managed not to get herself wet. Since she did it when your back was turned, it is not evident whether she was "fooling" while at the table or whether it was accidental.

If you were Kathie's mother, what would YOU do?

a. Try to find out how it happened and make her clean it up if she was to blame.

b. Clean up the mess yourself because you know she would not do a good job of it.

c. Point out to her the inconvenience and nuisance she causes you by such actions.

d. Punish her by depriving her of her milk for the rest of the week.

e. Let her clean it up and supervise her activity so that she does a competent job.

Edward Lettau

Discussion

Such accidents, intentional or otherwise, are what make mothers "blow their tops" sometimes. This is understandable. However, a consistent long-run policy for such expected accidents is necessary, and Kathie by now is old enough for alternative (e). (a) may develop into a prolonged cross-examination with attempted evasion or legitimate protestations of innocence. (d) is inadvisable because it tampers with the child's diet and may create eating problems. (b) and (c) go together and, if only to avoid the impression of complaining that (c) gives, you should avoid (b) and educate Kathie to policy (e) which can be used consistently with an older child. Moreover, it is a step in the right direction as far as self-sufficiency is concerned.

What Would You Do About
UNINTENTIONAL DESTRUCTIVENESS?

By RALPH K. MEISTER

Tony, age seven, was given a bow and arrow outfit with a target board set up in his own room. The arrows have rubber suction points to prevent injury but Tony brought the toy into the living room and after a few prelimary shots accidentally shot a small glass vase off its perch and onto the floor. Although the vase was neither priceless nor an heirloom it does represent a loss.

If you were Tony's mother what would YOU do?

(a) Make Tony clear up the pieces as punishment.

(b) Rule that Tony can only use the bow and arrow outdoors in the future.

(c) Confiscate all the arrows for a couple of weeks and restrict their future use to Tony's room and to the target board.

(d) Spank Tony for his carelessness.

(e) Do nothing to punish Tony since you were previously aware of the fact that he was shooting his arrows in the living room.

Discussion

When we put such a toy in the hands of a seven-year-old, it should be with specific, well-defined rules for its use. Outdoor use or use only with the target board are both good possibilities. However, since this "stitch-in-time" was not taken, alternative (c) is indicated. (e) points up our negligence but is scarcely a desirable way of handling the situation. Alternative (a) is not a sufficient punishment nor does it take care of possible future occurrences of this nature. (b), as mentioned above, may be a good rule but it does not include any punishment which does seem called for. Alternative (d)? This might supplement (c) if you are so provoked as to take it out on Tony some other way later on. However, the carelessness in this instance seems a joint responsibility— you should have spoken to Tony when he first came into the living room with the bow and arrows.

What Would You Do About
DIFFERING PARENTAL DECISIONS?

By RALPH K. MEISTER

Susan, age 8, has asked Mother whether she can visit a playmate in the neighborhood after dinner and Mother has refused. When Father comes home, Susan asks him and he says it is all right for her to go, provided she has an invitation from her friend's parents. Susan then confronts Mother with the fact that she has her father's permission.

If you were Susan's mother, what would YOU do?

(a) In deference to Father's decision, allow Susan to visit her friend.

(b) Refuse to let her go and take up later with Father the issue of countermanding your decision.

(c) Indicate to Susan that the first decision of either parent is the binding one so that she will not be tempted in the future to pit one against the other.

(d) Never make a decision without consultation by both parents.

H. Armstrong Roberts

(e) Punish Susan by deprivation of further visiting privileges during the week for having gone to her father after being denied by her mother.

Discussion

(d) is a good procedure for important issues affecting the child's future or welfare but is not particularly feasible for the thousand-and-one little items that come up in the course of everyday living. (b) is inappropriate because father has not consciously countermanded mother's decision. (a) is undesirable because it encourages this divisive behavior on Susan's part, and (e) is undesirable because it is too severe and punishment is not particularly called for. (c) would probably be best, pointing out to Susan that the parent denying her has reasons for doing so of which the other parent may be unaware. Therefore, the original decision must stand. Further, this ruling should dispose of such occurrences in the future. Only should Susan persist would we be justified in reconsidering alternative (d).

What Would You Do About PLAYTIME vs. DINNER?

By RALPH K. MEISTER

Mother has just called to Kathie and Dick to come in for dinner. Busily engaged in play, they have replied that they are not hungry.

If you were their mother, what would YOU do?

(a) Let them go without their dinner.

(b) Tell them to come into the house immediately "if they know what is good for them."

(c) Tell them they have ten more minutes to conclude their play.

(d) Promise them they can stay out later in the evening if they come in now.

(e) Insist that they come in even if they are not hungry.

Photograph by Harold M. Lambert

(f) Fix them a sandwich that they can eat without disturbing their play and so that they will be sure to have some evening nourishment.

Discussion

The attractiveness of play can often operate to minimize hunger pangs. However, it is not unreasonable for us to expect our children to be present for the evening meal. Therefore, a combination of (c) and (e) are to be recommended. If we insist consistently on their presence during the meal, they will almost always eat something. It is only when the avowal of no hunger gives them an indefinitely longer play time that they continue to use this tactic. (a) is inadvisable from the standpoint of their own health. If the decision is left to them, they will not at the moment want to stop their play for food even though they will be hungry later. The ten-minute or five-minute warning of (c) makes our insistence fair. The threat implicit in (b) is inadvisable because it may arouse resentment and really "spoil the appetite." (d) and (f) are unwholesome compromises. The use of (f) would soon establish the evening meal as an on-the-run sandwich affair. (d), even if it were effective in bringing them in (which is questionable) would merely create another problem at the bedtime end of the schedule. If we insist that they be present during the meal time without insisting necessarily that they eat and yet excuse them for evening play after they have finished eating, both the appetite and the play problem have the best chance for a happy solution.

What Would You Do About
HOME CHORES?

By RALPH K. MEISTER

Mother has asked Joanne, age nine, to help do the dinner dishes. Joanne is complaining because she expected to go out and play after dinner. However, mother feels her request is justified because she seldom asks Joanne to perform such household duties.

If you were Joanne's mother, what would YOU do?

(a) Insist that Joanne either help with the dishes or remain at home during the rest of the evening.

(b) Remind Joanne that the next time she requests a favor, a favorable answer to her request may not be forthcoming.

(c) Give Joanne a regular schedule of dish-washing so that she can plan

her time accordingly.

(d) Let her go out but impress upon her your disapproval of her attitude of unco-operativeness.

(e) Insist on her doing the dishes and, in addition, institute some reasonable punishment for her complaining.

Discussion

Unless the help we get from our children is given graciously, the entire issue is likely to be somewhat unpleasant for all concerned. Therefore, the best alternative as a general policy is alternative (c). It is somewhat frustrating to the child to be faced unexpectedly with a duty for which she had no opportunity to plan. Often matters do come up for which we have little warning, but even we adults do not always meet such unforeseen demands with perfect equanimity. Joanne's complaining, in this instance is not too unjustifiable. Therefore (d) and especially (e) would not be fair to the child. (b) is a not-too-subtle form of threatening and is undesirable for that reason. (a) is likely to evoke resentment but may be used if this particular instance is sufficiently important. Actually, all alternatives except (c) do contain a measure of punishment but (a) is the least objectionable in this respect, and (d) the most objectionable because it alienates both parties. Apart from the issue of discipline involved, a regular consistently-expected and not-overly-burdensome schedule of helping with household duties is a valuable educational measure for the child of all ages beyond the kindergarten level.

What Would You Do About
IRRESPONSIBILITY?

By RALPH K. MEISTER

Helen was asked to take care of baby brother Donald, age one and a half. While she was talking on the phone to a friend, he wandered away, fell, and bruised his face. Accused of playing instead of watching him, she gives a tearful denial.

If you were Helen's mother, what would YOU do?

(a) Punish her by making her take care of him for the next week.

(b) Deprive her of some play time for the next couple of days.

(c) Make her feel guilty for her neglect of him.

(d) Reprimand her for her absent-mindedness.

(e) Never let her take care of the baby again.

Ewing Galloway

Discussion

This is not a typical instance of the preoccupation of children this age. Helen should be reprimanded for her failure to pay closer attention to where the baby was going (d). However, (a) is not to be recommended because it may tend to engender some resentment against Donald if taking care of him is represented as punishment. (b) might be subject to this same objection. (c) and (e) are not advisable because guilt feelings are not an especially constructive approach to the problem. (d) is definitely indicated and should this not prove adequate on another occasion, (b) might also be used.

YOUR CHILD'S WORLD INDEX

M

Manners 101, 128
Marriage 39, 114
Meals 23, 93, 98, 123, 128, 153, 156
Mistakes of Parents 95
Morale 80
Mother 12, 14, 34, 108, 116, 132, 141, 151, 153, 155
Music 51, 77, 149

N

Nagging 7
Naps 44
Nature 64, 149
Neatness 122, 139
Neighbors 34, 67, 117, 122
Nighttime 46, 94, 108, 126, 129
Nine Years Old 157
"No" 27, 45, 68

O

Obedience 23, 49, 119, 124, 156

P

Parents 7, 10, 21, 23, 27, 29, 36, 80, 114, 128, 141, 149, 155
Permission 27, 29, 155
Play 57, 75, 87, 122, 127, 132, 149, 152, 156
Poetry 108
Possessions 61, 73
Preschool 31, 47, 57, 87, 143
Privacy 14
Promises 120
Punishment 23, 124, 154

Q

Question Asking 17, 47, 110

R

Reading 108, 141, 145, 147, 149
Repetitive Speech 72
Resentment 27, 158

Ritual 103
Rough Play 75, 76, 125, 127, 154
Running 67, 117

S

School 143, 145, 147
Scolding 84, 95, 119
Security 10
Self-Reliance 55, 149
Seven Years Old 151, 152, 153, 154
Sick Child 132
Six Years Old 121, 122, 123, 124, 125, 126, 127, 128, 129, 156
Slapping 96
Standards 87, 99
Sympathy 66, 129

T

Tantrums 42
Tattling 92
Teacher-Child Relationships 137, 141, 143
Television 137
Ten Months Old 42
Ten Years Old 158
Thankfulness 101
Three Years Old 71, 72, 73, 74, 75, 76
Toilet Training 23, 43
Toys 51, 71, 73, 76, 122, 154
Training 23, 43
Twenty-one Months Old 46
Two Years Old 66, 67, 68, 69, 70, 158

U

Understanding 12, 14, 64

V

Vocabulary 112

W

Washing 94, 139
What Would You Do? 42-46, 66-76, 89-98, 116-129, 151-158
Work Habits 53, 135, 157